THE MOVIE MUSICAL

QUICK TAKES: MOVIES AND POPULAR CULTURE

Quick Takes: Movies and Popular Culture is a series offering succinct overviews and high quality writing on cutting edge themes and issues in film studies. Authors offer both fresh perspectives on new areas of inquiry and original takes on established topics.

SERIES EDITORS:

Gwendolyn Audrey Foster is Willa Cather Professor of English and teaches film studies in the Department of English at the University of Nebraska, Lincoln.

Wheeler Winston Dixon is the James Ryan Endowed Professor of Film Studies and professor of English at the University of Nebraska, Lincoln.

Rebecca Bell-Metereau,
Transgender Cinema

Blair Davis,
Comic Book Movies

Jonna Eagle,
War Games

Lester D. Freidman,
Sports Movies

Desirée J. Garcia,
The Movie Musical

Steven Gerrard,
The Modern British Horror Film

Barry Keith Grant,
Monster Cinema

Julie Grossman,
The Femme Fatale

Daniel Herbert,
Film Remakes and Franchises

Ian Olney, *Zombie Cinema*

Valérie K. Orlando,
New African Cinema

Carl Plantinga,
Alternative Realities

Stephen Prince,
Digital Cinema

Dahlia Schweitzer,
L.A. Private Eyes

Steven Shaviro,
Digital Music Videos

David Sterritt,
Rock 'n' Roll Movies

John Wills, *Disney Culture*

The Movie Musical

DESIRÉE J. GARCIA

RUTGERS UNIVERSITY PRESS

New Brunswick, Camden, and Newark, New Jersey, and London

Library of Congress Cataloging-in-Publication Data
Names: Garcia, Desirée J., 1977– author.
Title: The movie musical / Desirée J. Garcia.
Description: New Brunswick : Rutgers University Press, 2021. |
Series: Quick takes: movies and popular culture |
Includes bibliographical references and index.
Identifiers: LCCN 2020010749 | ISBN 9781978803787 (paperback) |
ISBN 9781978803794 (hardcover) | ISBN 9781978803800 (epub) |
ISBN 9781978803817 (mobi) | ISBN 9781978803824 (pdf)
Subjects: LCSH: Musical films—United States—History
and criticism. | Musical films—History and criticism.
Classification: LCC PN1995.9.M86 G374 2021 |
DDC 791.43/6—dc23
LC record available at https://lccn.loc.gov/2020010749

A British Cataloging-in-Publication record for this book is
available from the British Library.

∞ The paper used in this publication meets the requirements of
the American National Standard for Information Sciences—
Permanence of Paper for Printed Library Materials,
ANSI Z39.48-1992.

www.rutgersuniversitypress.org

Manufactured in the United States of America

FOR EDIE BLUE

CONTENTS

Introduction 1

1 The Musical as Archive 15

2 The Musical as Society 49

3 The Musical as Mediation 79

Acknowledgments 115

Further Reading 117

References 123

Index 129

THE MOVIE MUSICAL

INTRODUCTION

The movie musical has had much to atone for over its history. Made possible by the film industry's embrace of sound cinema in the late 1920s, the creation of the movie musical appeared to signal the end of an era for the advancement of cinematic form. As Andrew Sarris observed in a 1977 essay, the new genre assumed cultural guilt as the "slayer of silent cinema" (quoted in O'Brien 2019, 2). Upon its inception and with the release of films like *The Jazz Singer* (Alan Crosland, 1927) and *Show Girl* (Alfred Santell, 1928), the musical was commonly viewed as the product of crass commercialism and bawdy sentimentality rather than intellectual engagement and aesthetic sophistication. This new category of cinema, defined according to its inclusion of singing and dancing to varying degrees and intents—a definitional schema that scholars have debated ever since (see Griffin 2018)—operated according to a logic of entertainment rather than art.

Fast-forward to the 1960s and the musical again came under fire as an inferior art form. The massive international hit that was *The Sound of Music* (Robert Wise,

1965) convinced the Hollywood studios that making more such musical blockbusters would produce the same enormous box-office receipts. When that scenario did not materialize as expected, so the narrative goes, the film studios experienced a massive recession, signaling an end to the "golden age" of Hollywood movies. Again, the commercialism and artificiality of the genre was to blame. Critics derisively called *The Sound of Music* "The Sound of Money" (*Variety* 1966). And Pauline Kael, in her now-infamous review of the film, referred to it as "the sugar-coated lie that people seem to want to eat," saying that it was "self-indulgent" and that it conjured "cheap and ready-made" responses from the public (1968).

For many decades, histories of Hollywood film framed *The Sound of Music* as the single film responsible for the near downfall of the studios and the genre itself. The subsequent musicals made in *The Sound of Music*'s image included *Camelot* (Joshua Logan, 1967), *Thoroughly Modern Millie* (George Roy Hill, 1967), *Doctor Dolittle* (Richard Fleischer, 1967), *Star!* (Robert Wise, 1968), *Funny Girl* (William Wyler, 1968), and *Hello, Dolly!* (Gene Kelly, 1969). When these films lost money, the viability of the musical came under question. Contemporary observers like the producer Cy Feuer countered this narrative, arguing that scores of people went to see these films, but their grossly inflated budgets prevented them from turning a profit (Tusher 1972). In recent decades, scholars have revised this history of crisis and downfall, including Steve Neale (2006), Brett Farmer (2010), Matthew Kennedy (2014), and Sean Griffin (2018), but the infamy that surrounds *The Sound of Music* and the movie musical in general lives on.

The Hollywood studios themselves have participated in the narrative that musicals are just fluff. One only has to recall Frank Sinatra's opening monologue to *That's Entertainment!* (Jack Haley Jr., 1974), a compilation film made up of musical numbers from MGM's golden age, the period from the 1930s to the 1950s. He faces the camera and states as a matter of fact, "Musicals were fantasy trips for the audiences of their day." "They may not tell you where our heads were at," he continues, "but they certainly tell you where our hearts were at." Pitched to 1970s audiences weary of political corruption, war, and racial conflict, *That's Entertainment!* fashioned itself as the means by which we could return to a simpler moment in time.

The criticism of the movie musical underlying all of these assessments of the genre is, of course, escapism. And it is the criticism with which *The Movie Musical* is most engaged not only because it has framed much of the genre's history to this point but also because it continues to be the dominant lens through which we encounter contemporary musicals. Escapism was the dominant critique of Damien Chazelle's *La La Land* (2016), which waxed nostalgic for Hollywood musicals and films from the golden age. Yet paradoxically, these same criticisms went hand in hand with taking the film to task for its representation of race and the authorship of black cultural forms like jazz (see Gabbard 2019; Cohan 2019b). So while *La La Land* was escapist and seemingly easily dismissed, many of its lay viewers spent significant time dissecting and critiquing the film as a central text in the debate about culture and representation.

I reference *La La Land* because it is emblematic of a paradox in the history of musical films: for all of their supposed irrelevance to the real world, musicals continue to be made and continue to be popular. Love them or hate them, evidence is everywhere that they appeal widely across various media and platforms. See, for example, the success of Randy Rainbow's YouTube channel, which he uses to perform numbers from musicals but with rewritten lyrics that comment on the contemporary political moment. Or consider the many shows on television that reproduce and regenerate the musical, such as reality contest shows (*American Idol*, 2002–; *So You Think You Can Dance*, 2005–; *The Voice*, 2011–), series like *Glee* (2009–15) and *Crazy Ex-Girlfriend* (2015–19) (see Kessler 2020). Videos of flash mobs, groups of people replicating song and dance scenes from *La La Land* and *The Greatest*

Showman, abounded on YouTube soon after the release of the films themselves. And annually, thousands of spectators gather in entertainment venues large and small to engage in improvised and orchestrated public sing-alongs for *The Rocky Horror Picture Show* (Jim Sharman, 1975), *The Sound of Music, Frozen* (Chris Buck and Jennifer Lee, 2013), and *The Greatest Showman* (Michael Gracey, 2017) (see Garcia 2014).

One problem of escapism as a critique is that it tends to end the discussion. It dismisses the genre without being thoughtful about why musicals continue to be made over and over again. We know from cultural theorists like Richard Dyer and Lawrence Levine that audiences do their escaping intentionally. As Dyer argues, musicals have never been "only entertainment," as they often serve the function of offering that which is lacking in our lives (2002, 23). When audiences choose the musical for their brand of escapism, as opposed to the escapism provided by other film genres or forms of popular culture, they determine, as Levine has argued, "what kinds of fictions, myths, fantasies they require, not primarily to escape reality but to face it day after day after day" (1992, 1375). In studying why audiences continue to support the musical, I have come to the conclusion that it is not about what audiences are running away from but what they are running toward.

Here I make an argument for the genre's continuity. In order to understand how and why the genre is still with us, we must get past the narratives of "crisis and rupture" that have persisted. With each new musical film to be released by the studios, critics announce that the musical may not be dead after all. In an internationally syndicated online article on Rappler.com, "A Musical Resurgence Has Hollywood Changing Its Tune," published on the heels of *La La Land*'s release, the writer declares that the "musical is taking center stage *once again* in Hollywood" and that Hollywood "is falling *back in love* with the movie musical" (2018; emphasis mine). The problems here are twofold. First, the article suggests that the musical fell out of favor at some point but now has returned to a place of cultural acceptance. And second, the article focuses exclusively on Hollywood and therefore does not take into account the histories of musical film traditions and international auteurs engaged with the genre that have persisted across time. Part of the issue is one of definition, as Sean Griffin has observed: "there has been far too much emphasis on the comfort of the familiar structure of the integrated musical, and not enough celebration of liberation from that definition" (2018, 8). Writing a history of the American film musical from its origins to the present, Griffin demonstrates how "the film musical has survived ably, by evolving into new patterns and structures regardless of attempts to keep it locked in place" (8). This volume takes up Griffin's project of demonstrating the elasticity of the genre beyond the period of Hollywood's golden age. But I am also interested in considering the genre more broadly as an international one and one made by directors who have been historically underrepresented in Hollywood's production of musicals, including women, Latinx film-makers, and black filmmakers. To do so requires a revisioning of the genre's historiography and a reckoning with the way the genre's history has been told within Hollywood-centric paradigms.

To be sure, scholars have initiated discussions about the movie musical in other cultural traditions and contexts. In the edited collections by Corey K. Creekmur and Linda K. Mokdad (2013) and Steven Cohan (2010), a range of scholars analyze musicals from multiple countries and over time. The call to rewrite the genre's history with an acknowledgment of international production has been made by Adrian Martin (2003), Sangita Gopal and Sujata Moorti (2011), Björn Norðfjörð (2013), Caryl Flinn (2016), Charles O'Brien (2019), and Kathryn Kalinak (2019). I contributed to this body of work with my previous book, *The Migration of Musical Film: From Ethnic Margins to American Mainstream* (2014). Continuing in this vein, *The Movie Musical* treats the genre capaciously; it places Hollywood classics, independently produced films, and musicals from around the world in the same conversation.

Battling the notion that the genre's escapism renders it meaningless to the real world, I divide this volume into three thematically organized chapters: the musical as archive; the musical as society; and the musical as mediation. In each, I investigate the ability of the genre to adapt to changing times, cultures, and audiences. Examples span from the earliest movie musicals in the 1920s to the present day in order to show continuities and shifts in form and narrative. And the thematic orientation of the book allows me to consider how the genre's language manifests change and continuity across modes of production and geographic boundaries as well.

In chapter 1, "The Musical as Archive," I examine the musical's ability to make a case for itself to new audiences by functioning as its own archive. In other words, the musical documents its own history and uses its own historical materials to interpret its present. The earliest musicals house and revive past entertainment forms, such as vaudeville, musical comedy, and minstrelsy, in order to revel in nostalgia but also to demonstrate that like the amusements of yesteryear, modern musicals are entertaining too. As musical films evolved, they archived past musicals, such as in *Singin' in the Rain* (Stanley Donen and Gene Kelly, 1952). Archival references cross national boundaries as well. *La La Land* is a particularly rich example of a Hollywood musical that quotes from earlier Hollywood musicals like the Astaire-Rogers films; Chazelle's first musical film, *Guy and Madeline on a Park Bench* (2009); and French musicals like Jacques Demy's *The Umbrellas of Cherbourg* (1964) and *The Young Girls of Rochefort* (1967). In *La La Land*'s case, the film self-consciously states its own genealogy, a genealogy that looks backward in order to find a path forward.

But perhaps the most intriguing instances of archiving have come from outside the United States. Jane Feuer has argued that films like *Strictly Ballroom* (Australia; Baz Luhrmann, 1992), *Everyone Says I Love You* (US independent; Woody Allen, 1996), *Shall We Dance* (Japan; Masayuki Suo, 1996), *Little Voice* (United Kingdom; Mark Herman, 1998), *Dancer in the Dark* (Denmark; Lars von Trier, 2000), and *Billy Elliot* (Stephen Daldry, 2000) are a subgenre of the musical proper, the international art musical. They share in the impulse to reference earlier Hollywood musicals but from a significant distance. "Instead of representing the lead performers in old Hollywood musicals," Feuer argues, the main characters "take up the position of spectators of old Hollywood musicals in a world where it is no longer possible to be Fred Astaire" (2010, 55). These musical films, in other words, catalog the spectatorship of movie musicals, demonstrating that, no matter how different lived reality is from the musical's realm of fantasy, the genre still provides something generative. This archival project in which musicals reference other musicals (and musicals reference forms of movie-musical spectatorship) has been a critical means by which the genre makes itself relevant to new audiences around the globe. In the films I discuss here, the characters' worlds recall and temporarily resemble the qualities of song and dance sequences, only to return again to stark reality. But these moments are strategically important to surviving those realities, as when the female character in *The Hole* (Ming-liang Tsai, 1998) imagines a life away from death and disease or when the animals in *The Burden* (Niki Lindroth Von Bahr, 2017) give musical expression to their feelings of anomie. As John Limon has argued about contemporary directors' use of *The Sound of Music* in globalized contexts of production, "escapism is where one goes to find what is inescapable" (2016, 51). In *The Hole* and *The Burden*, the musical is both pleasure and pain. These musicals and many others reveal how the desire to escape and the inability to do so represent a persistent narrative theme that finds its inspiration in present-day conditions.

In chapter 2, "The Musical as Society," I take on the issue of authorship. If one were to focus exclusively on Hollywood, it would be easy to dismiss movie musicals as the products of a white male subjectivity. In telling stories about women, immigrants, and peoples of color, Hollywood musicals have consistently placed the reins of control in the hands of people who do not share those perspectives. If we look beyond Hollywood, however, we can find examples of filmmakers from marginalized positions in society who have used the musical genre as a means of critiquing society. This chapter begins with a discussion of how the Hollywood musical has identified social issues directly. It refutes the claim that the genre does not engage in social critique by using examples of musicals that address assimilation, including treatments of immigration and ethnicity (in *The Jazz Singer*, Alan Crosland, 1927, for example), intolerance toward the working classes (in films like *Gold Diggers of 1933*, Mervyn LeRoy, 1933; and *Babes in Arms*, Busby Berkeley, 1939), and the distrust of social outsiders (*The Music Man*, Morton DaCosta, 1962). But this chapter goes further to focus on musicals made outside and, in some cases, in defiance of the Hollywood model. The majority of the chapter analyzes three films that take the backstage musical, which tells stories about performers' lives, as the means by which to revise the spectacularized representations and framings of Mexican Americans, black Americans, and women. The directors Luis Valdez (*La Bamba*, 1987), Spike Lee (*Bamboozled*, 2000), and Sally Potter (*The

Tango Lesson, 1997) appropriate the backstage musical in order to tell stories about ethnicity, race, and gender, respectively, in ways that upend the genre's conventions that have alternately stereotyped and constrained representations of marginalized groups. Far from escapist, these interventions demonstrate the musical's elasticity as a form and its ability to grapple with the complexities of social relations.

Chapter 3, "The Musical as Mediation," assesses the genre's relationship to media and technology over time and space. While the musical is rarely the genre that comes to mind when we think about forms of mediation, its self-consciousness as an inheritor of past entertainment forms has prompted recognition of how new technologies, namely, sound cinema, have produced new forms, of which the musical is one. The genre's nostalgic impulse, most developed by the folk musical subgenre, has repeatedly shown an investment in demonstrating how once-new forms of technology in the past (the telephone, the trolley, the automobile) can be integrated into the project of holding families together and strengthening communities rather than weakening them.

Chapter 3 foregrounds the Irish filmmaker John Carney's films *Once* (2007), *Begin Again* (2013), and *Sing Street* (2016) as examples of musicals that employ mediation extensively in their narrative structure and form.

Featuring main characters who are musicians rather than performers, Carney's films insist on the experience of music, creating it, listening to it, and playing it, in contemporary contexts. And he demonstrates the multiple ways that music can be a mediating device for human connection. He foregrounds the materiality of print, broadcast, and recording media, in both analog and digital forms, to facilitate these interpersonal connections. His musicals offer an experience of mediated communion that overcomes modern ills such as the allure of celebrity and consumerism (*Begin Again*), the sense of social dislocation wrought by immigration (*Once, Begin Again*), and divorce and teenage angst (*Sing Street*).

As this is a "quick take" on the musical, *The Movie Musical* cannot possibly cover all relevant examples of the points discussed here. With a thematic rather than chronological approach, I have tried to indicate some alternate approaches to the history of the movie musical that highlight its longevity as a highly adaptable and resilient cinematic language. And in order to make this volume an accessible point of entry for the study of the genre, I have deliberately chosen examples of films that are accessible on either DVD or streaming media so that students inside and outside the classroom can read it alongside the films themselves. Moreover, with its expansive periodization and its emphasis on musicals made

outside Hollywood, I intend for this book to complement other studies of the musical already in existence.
While entertainment and pleasure will always be associated with the genre, it is my hope that we can continue to
approach the musical, in all of its diversity, with both our
hearts and our heads.

1

THE MUSICAL AS ARCHIVE

There is a moment toward the beginning of *La La Land*, Damien Chazelle's 2016 original film musical, when the two main characters explore a Hollywood back lot. Mia (Emma Stone) guides Sebastian (Ryan Gosling) through the space as film crews adjust scenes and props enter in and out of soundstages. It is a dynamic set that shows the functioning of a Hollywood studio. *La La Land* is a recent iteration of a "back-studio" picture, movies about the process of making movies that, as Steven Cohan says, "demystify the production of entertainment as a condition for remystifying it" (2019a, 2). This particular back-lot sequence at once demonstrates the kinds of activities that go on behind the scenes while reaffirming the movies as magical and glamorous. As the characters walk, Mia expresses her love for classic Hollywood films and her desire to be an actress one day. Seb, too, discusses his passion for jazz and his ambition to open his own club. Theirs is an earnest conversation that the false landscape around them places in harsh relief. As the back-studio picture does so well, *La La Land* suggests that for all of its artificiality, this genre still has the power to inspire and nurture one's dreams.

The self-reflexive qualities that are at the heart of the back-studio picture also structure the musical. Indeed, like *La La Land*, many back-studio pictures are musicals themselves or involve musical numbers (*Singin' in the Rain*, Stanley Donen and Gene Kelly, 1952; *A Star Is Born*, George Cukor, 1954; *Hollywood Shuffle*, Robert Townsend, 1987; *The Artist*, Michel Hazanavicius, 2011; *Hail, Caesar!*, Ethan and Joel Coen, 2016). In the scene just described, Chazelle references the history of musical film at multiple times and on multiple levels. Most directly, the scene is reminiscent of a similar one in *Singin' in the Rain*, when Don (Gene Kelly) and Kathy (Debbie Reynolds) walk through the back lot of Monumental Pictures. Like Mia and Sebastian, Don and Kathy are just getting to know each other. The film shows the inner workings of the studio, a series of soundstages and moving props, providing an exploration of the liminal space between reality and fantasy; as such, the scene provides a reflection on how the musical often converges the two realms. As Don sings to Kathy in the "You Are My Lucky Star" number, he employs the studio effects of light, wind, and painted backdrop to help him express his heartfelt emotions.

Like *Singin' in the Rain* before it, *La La Land* is as invested in telling a story about romance as it is in exploring its own relationship to the musical film. In the earlier film, the process of making a musical film becomes the focus of the characters' energies; in order to save their film in the wake of the sound revolution, they must make a musical that captures the excitement surrounding another (in some ways the first) musical film, *The Jazz Singer* (Alan Crosland, 1927). In *La La Land*, the studio back-lot scene reveals how the film is equally indebted to, and in dialogue with, other musical films. For a brief moment, Mia and Seb pause in front of a studio warehouse in which gaffers and grips prepare a scene for shooting. The scene shows the two characters as they gaze at the activity while studio workers pull a large billboard on a dolly behind them. The image is a movie poster for a film called *Guy and Madeline*, a shortened version of the title of Damien Chazelle's first narrative feature and film musical, *Guy and Madeline on a Park Bench* (2009).

The parallels between *La La Land* and *Guy and Madeline on a Park Bench* are many. They both place jazz, its performance and its longevity as an art form, at the forefront of the narrative. They explore the themes of romance and the conflicts posed by individual ambition. And the main characters are a male jazz musician (piano in *La La Land*, trumpet in *Guy and Madeline*) and a female restaurant worker (a barista in *La La Land*, a waitress in *Guy and Madeline*). While the modes of production are at odds— Chazelle's earlier film started out as a student production while he was enrolled at Harvard University, had a small budget, and aesthetically aligned itself more with independent and avant-garde aesthetics (nonprofessional actors, discontinuous editing, handheld camera, black-and-white film stock), whereas *La La Land* is a glossy studio production with major Hollywood stars—the similarities between the two films suggest a continuity in Chazelle's work that he himself acknowledges by inserting *Guy and Madeline* directly into *La La Land's* back-lot scene.

Finally, this particular moment in *La La Land* points not just to Hollywood musicals of old and the director's earlier work but to musicals made outside the United States. Chazelle first gives us a reference to Jacques Demy's *Les parapluies de Cherbourg* (*The Umbrellas of Cherbourg*, 1964) toward the beginning of the scene as Mia and Seb start their walk. When Mia directs Seb's gaze to the building across from her coffee shop, which "Humphrey Bogart and Ingrid Bergman looked out of in *Casablanca*," we notice that the first floor of that building is an umbrella (*parapluies*) shop nearly identical to the one in Demy's film.

La La Land also gestures toward non-Hollywood musicals with the *Guy and Madeline* billboard. Despite the film title, the billboard image is not from Chazelle's first film. Instead, it portrays a close-up of a man and a woman gazing romantically toward each other against a nightscape of stars and framed by orange groves. The image contrasts sharply with the look and feel of Chazelle's first musical. And it is equally at odds with the musicals of classical Hollywood, which it nonetheless references with the bylines "All Singing! All Dancing!" and "In Technicolor," phrases historically used by the studios to indicate a film's status as a musical to movie audiences. Instead, the image is exotic looking due to the graphics (which use an *Arabian Nights*–style font) and to the depiction of the two central characters, whose dark skin tones differ from those of the *La La Land* protagonists who stand in front of it. Like the reference to *Les parapluies de Cherbourg* earlier in the scene, the billboard is an admission that musicals are part of the past *and* present, made both domestically and throughout the world. Chazelle emphasizes the global reach of musical film with the prominent placement of a large world globe in the scene, the only prop left outside the stage set that the billboard passes.

Making note of the film's many intra- and intertextual references in just this one scene constitutes the first steps toward a cinematic genealogy that can be mapped through time and space of musical film history. As we see in the back-lot sequence, musicals are dynamic, and they are transnational. They cross-fertilize one another over geographic and national borders. These qualities are not peculiar to *La La Land*, which is merely a recent example of how the musical continuously self-references in direct and indirect ways. The musical persistently quotes itself, having characters discuss other musical films, characters, and stars, and it recalls entertainment forms associated with earlier eras like jazz, Tin Pan Alley, tap, and ballroom dance. The musical is, in essence, an archive in which a repository of cultural information is held and accessed by successive iterations of the genre. A film like *La La Land*, in other words, reaches back in order to move forward. It makes a case for itself as a musical by demonstrating, in entertaining fashion, how the qualities of other musicals continue to be relevant today. In this way, the musical's archival impulse makes possible its regeneration for new audiences.

Expounding on Jane Feuer's foundational theories regarding the genre's self-reflexive operation, including its reliance on pastiche and hybridity, the notion of an archive gets at central questions perpetually raised by critics and fans: After all these years, why does the musical continue to be popular? What accounts for its resilience? And how is it able to resonate with shifting audience tastes and attitudes? As the first original musical film to be made by the Hollywood studios in years, *La La Land* was an enormous success with critics and the public. As I have suggested, however, it is also a nexus of musical-film crosscurrents and intentionally so. *La La Land* is the vestigial embodiment of these many cinematic references and brings them into the twenty-first century as an otherwise original work.

In assessing the musical's uniqueness among genres, Barry Keith Grant observes that the musical is the only genre that "consistently violates the otherwise rigid logic of classic narrative cinema. . . . The sudden injection of song and dance into a narrative always announces the work's own artifice" (2012, 3–4). The disruptive powers of performance, embedded via various formal techniques into the otherwise "closed system" of the film narrative, open up the possibilities for audience engagement with the genre. First and foremost, the inclusion of the audience itself as a character in such films is a structuring feature that renders it deeply self-conscious as a cultural form. But self-reflexivity has also given it a paradoxical place in Hollywood history. While it has always been "the least classical" of Hollywood films, the musical has also been the "quintessential Hollywood product," as Feuer has pointed out: "all Hollywood films manipulated audience response, but the musical could incorporate that response into the film itself; all Hollywood films sought to be entertaining, but the musical could incorporate a myth of entertainment into its aesthetic discourse" (2002, 38). It is unlike other classical Hollywood genres because of the disruptive power of its song and dance sequences, but those same performative moments provide the space for metacommentary on the musical itself, Hollywood, and entertainment writ large.

In the genre's evolution inside and outside Hollywood, we can see the many ways in which the musical's archival impulse serves the needs of the present. While the musical's themes, style, and tone have shifted over nearly one hundred years of production, its quotation of itself provides continuity in the face of change; historically, the genre has reveled in nostalgia, forming a community out of individuals, integration out of alienation (Feuer 1982; Dyer 2002; Garcia 2014). In creating the sense that musicals are always with us, providing a ritual function of bringing the past into the present, the genre makes an argument for its own endurance.

This chapter examines three ways in which the musical archives itself. First, it reflects on how and where the quotations of other musicals and musical-film stars appear, beginning with examples from the early sound era to the present. Second, the chapter examines the genre's quotation and reconciliation of older cultural forms with newer ones in order to demonstrate how pastiche and hybridity are central to how the musical perpetuates itself for contemporary audiences. And finally, the chapter explores how the musical uses its self-reflexive moments in order to address present-day problems and concerns.

QUOTATION

To some extent, all genre films rely on quotation of others in the genre. As Christian Metz observes, a genre is an "infinite text" that repeats formulas and engages in repetition (1974, 152). And for genres with great longevity, like the western, such formulas and repetitions extend deep into our historical experience. Certainly, there are moments of profound self-reflexivity in certain genre films, like the quotation of *On the Waterfront* (Elia Kazan, 1954) in *Raging Bull* (Martin Scorsese, 1980), of *Angels with Dirty Faces* (Michael Curtiz, 1938; retitled as "Angels with Filthy Faces") in *Home Alone* (Chris Columbus, 1990), and of *The Graduate* (Mike Nichols, 1967) in *500 Days of Summer* (Marc Webb, 2009), to name just a few. But no other genre carries with it the vestiges of its own history like the musical. In a process of "growth through recycling," the musical makes references to itself as a matter of course and as a matter of survival (Feuer 1982, 93).

For example, one popular touchstone for the movie musical is the iconic song-and-dance team Fred Astaire and Ginger Rogers. As stars of RKO musicals in the 1930s, they combined the performance of ballroom dance with acts of courtship and romantic love (Cohan 2002, 93). And as Edward Gallefant has pointed out, "among the famous star couples of the 'thirties and 'forties, they are the only pair (still) popularly known by their first names" (2002, 6). Their entwined, swirling bodies have reverberated through movie musicals of different eras, in the United States and abroad, as symbols of elegance and desire. And in each subsequent iteration of the duo, the connection between musicals of the past and musicals of the present becomes further solidified.

The first self-reflexive posturing of the Astaire-Rogers team came from Astaire and Rogers themselves. By 1939, they had made eight musicals together and were a household name nearly synonymous with the musical itself. That year, they made their ninth film, *The Story of Vernon and Irene Castle*, a biopic about the eponymous dancing team from the early twentieth century. This film, their last until ten years later, resurrected the dance and clothing styles that the Castles had made famous decades earlier for 1930s audiences. Significantly, however, in retelling the Castles' story, Astaire and Rogers also memorialized their own. Their look back onto a moment of cultural origin when a previous couple made dance history cannot help but reference their own accomplishments as a dancing team, who by 1939 had redefined dance onscreen and the musical film itself. Their subsequent film, *The Barkleys of Broadway* (Charles Walters, 1949), was, in turn, a story of a married couple whose careers in show business, and musical comedy, have been intertwined for years. As Feuer writes, this particular film uses "intertextuality and star iconography" to evoke nostalgia for the dancing couple's earlier films and performance routines (2002, 37). It also communicated that the Astaire-and-Rogers-type entertainment was still entertaining and that, perhaps more importantly, the musical film was still alive and well. As with *Singin' in the Rain*, the musical saves the day; its allure as a form of entertainment woos Ginger Rogers's character back to the musical stage and back to the arms of her husband (Astaire). In the end, as with all backstage musicals about putting on a show, the "myth of entertainment" is upheld (Feuer 2002, 31). Musical entertainment and the musical itself are the unblemished heroes of such narratives.

But if the entertainment value of the Hollywood musical is indeed a myth, it has enjoyed an impressive afterlife, and it is one that successive generations of filmmakers and audiences have continued to express belief in. If we move beyond the historical moment of classical Hollywood (1930–60) and its industrial mode of production, we see that the Astaire-and-Rogers dancing team continues to be quoted across an array of musicals. Here I would include Federico Fellini's film *Ginger and Fred* (1986), in which an aging dancing couple reunite for a nostalgic variety show on Italian television, *We Are Proud to Present*. Much of the film anticipates the meeting between Amelia, played by Fellini's wife, the actress Giulietta Masina, and Pippo, played by Marcello Mastroianni. The narrative features a series of interrupted rehearsals and recollections of their glory days and builds toward the ultimate moment on Christmas Eve when Amelia and Pippo perform onstage. With nods to Fellini's earlier work in which both Masina and Mastroianni starred, the film is laden with intertextual moments. Its allusion to Astaire and Rogers, however, is perhaps the most overt form of quotation of the past. As the story goes, Amelia and Pippo achieved fame by impersonating Astaire and Rogers, and like that dancing team, their act broke up in 1939. For their reunion, they wore the iconic costumes of Astaire and Rogers in *Top Hat* (Mark Sandrich, 1935), a top hat and tails for Pippo and a plumed and sequined gown for Amelia (*Swing Time*, George Stevens, 1936). For the couple and the film itself, Astaire and Rogers represent a simpler and happier time. But while Amelia looks forward to reuniting with her old partner, she meets with constant disappointment. Pippo is now forgetful and physically weary. He gets winded while rehearsing, and he often acts inconsiderately toward Amelia, crudely showing interest in other women in front of her. The television show is a garish amalgam of sex, gluttony, and materialism despite the religious overtones of the holiday proper. Pippo rails against the audience who flock like sheep to television programming. Even their anticipated performance is initially disheartening. Pippo becomes disoriented and forgets the steps. Threatening their dance further, a power outage interrupts their routine and forces them to wait on a darkened studio stage until the lights turn back on.

Consistent with backstage musicals of an earlier era, however, the show goes on. The performers overcome the hurdles placed in front of them, and they muster through to give an entertaining performance. As they bow to their audience, Amelia and Pippo smile knowing that they have convinced the audience and themselves that they can still conjure the "Ginger and Fred" of yore. The final scene of the film occurs at a train station where they say good-bye not with words but with the opening part of their act: Pippo makes the sound of an ocean-liner horn about to depart, and Amelia throws her arms up and exclaims his name. Despite the crudeness around them and the difficulties of old age, the quotation of their earlier selves, which are a simulation of the actual Astaire-Rogers dancing team, allows them a space for beauty and romance once again.

Ten years later, the comedian and filmmaker Woody Allen recalled the Astaire-Rogers number to lend a magical aura to his original musical film *Everyone Says I Love You*. His film draws on a number of musical-film traditions, including a celebration of the seasons (the folk musical), the use of song and dance to create community among strangers (Ernst Lubitsch; Rouben Mamoulian) and to inspire courtship (Astaire-Rogers films), and a vacillation between diegetic and nondiegetic music to demarcate and integrate musical performance into the narrative.

Like *Ginger and Fred*, Astaire and Rogers enter into Allen's musical to add poignance to the end of a relationship. Joe (Woody Allen) and Steffi (Goldie Hawn) are divorced but remain friends as their families celebrate Christmas Eve together in Paris. And like Fellini's film, the holiday serves as a ritualistic occasion to gather and reflect on one's memories. The divorcees find themselves walking along the Seine and reminiscing about what went right and what went wrong with their relationship. She begins to sing their song, "I'm Through with Love," while he quietly listens. At the end of one verse, they begin to dance. Their movements conjure those of Astaire and Rogers's ballroom dances. And the overall structure of the number, from song to dance to the couple holding hands while they walk as pedestrians once more, recalls any number of Astaire-Rogers sequences, such as "Smoke Gets in Your Eyes" in *Roberta* (William A. Seiter, 1935) and "Pick Yourself Up" in *Swing Time*.

Allen's comical addition of flying dance movements, in which Steffi's part of the dance becomes airborne while a surprised Joe looks on, is also a reference to the earlier dancing team. Musical numbers, as Astaire choreographed and performed them, were moments of elation set apart from the humdrum realism of the story. They are magical moments when the narrative takes a pause. This feeling of suspended movement makes for fantastical suspensions of time and space in otherwise-plausible, cause-and-effect narratives. Allen's evocation that Steffi becomes weightless is at once a comical nod to the fact that Allen cannot dance (much less lift) and a means of placing his own film in dialogue with musicals that have come before. With this number, he is especially invested in maintaining the myth of entertainment that allows for anything to happen inside a performance number, where ordinary people can suddenly do extraordinary things.

Defying gravity is essential to a later quotation of Astaire and Rogers: Chazelle's *La La Land*. Setting the

stage for the transcendent musical number "Planetar-
ium," Chazelle chose the Griffith Observatory, itself a
reference to a film that is quoted within the narrative at
multiple points, *Rebel without a Cause* (Nicholas Ray,
1955). But unlike the scene in that earlier film in which
disaffected teenagers get a lesson in planetary science,
Chazelle's use of the observatory has a romantic impulse:
to take Mia and Seb to the stars. Like so many Astaire-
Rogers moments that have come before, the dance number achieves the romantic consummation of the two
main characters. In a whimsical moment, Seb lifts Mia,
and she floats upward into the sky, where he joins her
and they dance ballroom-style. Once they initiate the
number, they turn into silhouettes of themselves, a tech-
nique that Astaire used in *Swing Time*. While it is clear
that the silhouettes are of two professional dancers sub-
stituting for Emma Stone and Ryan Gosling, the choice
is part of a larger set of conceits to achieve the sense of
fantasy that courtship and love and song and dance can
provide. In using silhouettes, moreover, Chazelle raises
the number to the level of the symbolic. The dancers
become faceless approximations of all other dancing
couples in all other musical films, most obviously referencing Astaire and Rogers. Lest we think that dancing in
the stars is unique to *La La Land*, it bears remembering
that Astaire and Rogers did it first, significantly, in their

first film that iconized their stardom, *The Story of Vernon and Irene Castle.*

While too numerous to list here, many other musicals archive their relationship to Astaire and Rogers or to Astaire himself (such as *Easter Parade,* 1948; *The Tango Lesson,* 1997; and *Billy Elliot,* 2000) as a means of signaling the film's genealogical connections to musicals of the past. The list of references becomes even longer if we include instances of nonmusical films enlisting the resilient appeal of musical-film spectatorship, as in Woody Allen's *The Purple Rose of Cairo* (1985), and the ability of love to overcome otherwise-prohibitive barriers of difference, as in Guillermo del Toro's monster film *The Shape of Water* (2017).

The tendency toward quotation in musical film also extends beyond allusions to Astaire and Rogers. The earliest backstage musicals of the 1930s referenced past entertainment forms that were both precursors to the musical film and an integral component of it, like musical comedy, minstrelsy, and vaudeville. French filmmakers like Jean-Luc Godard (*A Woman Is a Woman,* 1961) and Jacques Demy (*The Young Girls of Rochefort,* 1967) make direct references to and even cast Gene Kelly in their films. Kelly also appears as a version of himself in the 1980s roller-skating musical *Xanadu* (Robert Greenwald, 1980). The makers of *Grease* (Randal Kleiser, 1978) cast icons of musicals past Joan Blondell and Frankie Avalon as adult characters who educate the teenagers in the film. A working-class man in Sheffield, England, cites Donald O'Connor as his inspiration for becoming a musical performer in *The Full Monty* (Peter Cattaneo, 1997). Yves Montand plays himself in the last film by Demy, *Trois places pour le 26* (*Three Seats for the 26th*, 1988), in which the actor triumphantly returns to the place of his birth with a musical show that is once again a hit. And Judy Garland appears on the soundtrack of Terence Davies's musical exploration of his youth, *The Long Day Closes* (1992), and in the song lyrics of Chazelle's first musical film, *Guy and Madeline on a Park Bench*. And even an unsentimental rock musical like *Tommy* (Ken Russell, 1975) positions itself as an inheritor of the earlier rock musicals *Bye Bye Birdie* (George Sidney, 1963) and *Viva Las Vegas* (George Sidney, 1964) by casting Ann-Margret in the role of the sexy but irresponsible mother.

In all of these musicals, the impulse to look backward and cite musicals and musical stars of the past is a significant part of the narrative. And while they all make a case for the value of entertainment in our lives, they also make an argument for the value of movie musicals in the present moment. Beyond conjuring romance and glamour, the quotation of musicals past demonstrates how they offer tools for meeting the concerns of today. And one central way in which they do so is through the explicit discussion and assessment of the value of old entertainment forms versus new ones.

PASTICHE AND HYBRIDITY

In 1998, the film theorist Fredric Jameson pointed to the ways that popular culture had become increasingly self-conscious in the age of late capitalism, the 1970s–1990s, when globalized and transnational communication flows set loose a "vast world-wide disembodied phantasmagoria" (1998, 142). Pastiche, the simulation and the recycling of past cultural forms, and hybridity, the anachronistic juxtaposition of old forms and new, became hallmarks of a culture that, as *La La Land*'s Seb says about people in Los Angeles (in many ways, the most postmodern of cities), "they worship everything and they value nothing." *Ginger and Fred* is one such postmodern text with its anachronistic use of the elegant Astaire-Rogers image amid the gaudy and garish world of 1980s Italian television. While postmodernism references intertextuality, pastiche, and hybridity in a specific, late twentieth-century historical moment, there are cultural forms, like the musical film, that have been self-referential since their beginning. Those musicals of the 1970s and '80s that we consider to have postmodern qualities, like *Tommy* (1975), *The Rocky Horror Picture Show* (Jim Sharman, 1975), *All That Jazz* (Bob Fosse, 1979), *Pennies from Heaven* (Herbert Ross, 1981), and *Ginger and Fred*, extend, accentuate, and amplify the genre's self-reflexive qualities rather than introduce them. Always the "least classical" of Hollywood genres, the musical's relationship to self-reflexivity has resulted in its elasticity over time; it bears within its very structure the ability to comment on itself as an art form and as a cultural product according to the needs of each successive generation. To be sure, these later musicals reflect the tenor of their time; they project a cynical attitude toward forms of heteronormative virtue and authority. And they recast the 1930s not in the image of Hollywood glamour but, rather, as in *Pennies from Heaven*, as a moment of social crisis, vapidity, and hedonism. But even these musicals ultimately rest on the power of musical performance as a tool for self-expression and to position the musical film as a viable cultural form in the present. The integration of rock 'n' roll into the narrative of musical film in *Tommy* and *Rocky Horror Picture Show*, demonstrating that the musical can adapt and change to new audience tastes, is a case in point (Grant 1986, 199).

Over the course of the genre's history, it has used the tools of pastiche and hybridity in order to ask and then answer the perpetual question, Will the musical still be entertaining? Featuring examples of older cultural forms and placing them alongside and in competition with newer ones, the musical conserves the history of its own formation and then integrates that history into a narrative about the musical in the present. In the process, the genre addresses the needs of a society in flux, acknowledging that change is ever a reality but that musical entertainment and the musical film can help us to meet and attenuate the unsettling shifts of time.

The musical achieves this through implicit and explicit ways. Biopics, many of which are musicals by virtue of their focus on musical celebrities, achieve this implicitly. Narrative features about the lives of past performers double as period films that reconstitute the past for the purposes of the present. An early biopic, *Somebody Loves Me* (Irving Brecher, 1952), starring Betty Hutton as the real-life vaudeville star Blossom Seeley, reconciled the career ambitions of its female protagonist with the concerns about women and domesticity in the postwar era. In 1972, Diana Ross embodied Billie Holiday in the Motown-produced *Lady Sings the Blues* (Sidney J. Furie, 1972), which not only reinterpreted Holiday's music for new generations but also recast black Americans as central to the nation's musical history. And in 2017, Hugh Jackman produced a musical version of the life of the nineteenth-century showman P. T. Barnum in *The Greatest Showman*

(Michael Gracey, 2017), which drastically rewrote Barnum's history in order tell a motivational story about accepting multiple forms of social difference.

Going back further, the first musical films, including *The Jazz Singer* (1927), *Sally* (1929), and *The Broadway Melody* (1929), took as their subject the production of other entertainment forms like musical comedy and vaudeville. In *The Jazz Singer*, the musical-comedy stage is a site of upward mobility and self-expression for the Jewish immigrant Jakie Rabinowitz. In *Sally*, Marilyn Miller performs her star turn in the real-life Broadway hit *Sally*, a Ziegfeld show that itself celebrates the star-making power of Ziegfeld shows. And in *The Broadway Melody*, a sister act aspires to make a life for themselves in show business. By featuring live entertainment forms so prominently in the narrative, these backstage musicals make an argument for their continued viability. They did so, ironically, just as the musical film was usurping the popularity of other entertainments and the Hollywood studios were converting existing theaters into movie palaces. The backstage musical film coalesces the past and present, demonstrating how musicals on the screen not only perpetuate what is good about the past but also deliver entertainment that is as good or better.

While biopics and the backstage musical film introduce performers and performances of the past to contemporary audiences, there is a large body of musical films that insists on discussing the merits of old versus new entertainment forms more directly. An early example is the musical-film short *Every Sunday* (Felix E. Feist, 1936), in which the child stars Judy Garland (as Judy) and Deanna Durbin (as Edna) combine their vocal talents to save the bandstand orchestra in their neighborhood park. Judy initiates the number, singing the song "Americana" in waltz time and with a belabored manner. Suddenly, she begins scatting the song and looking directly at the camera. The film cuts in this moment from a medium-long shot that positions her against the elderly classical musicians behind her to a medium close-up in which her figure fills the frame. The number vacillates in and out of these two framings, corresponding to her scatting interludes, until she begins to encourage the musicians to play the song in swing time rather than as a waltz. In response to the new energy coming from the bandstand, couples of all generations begin to hold hands and sway to the music, and people begin rushing into the park. For the last part of the song, Edna joins Judy. This time, the two alternate between scatting (Judy) and operatic trilling (Edna), culminating in the complete integration of their respective vocal strengths for the chorus of the number.

This scene in *Every Sunday* communicates how musical film justifies its own brand of entertainment. On the one hand, Judy must liven up the orchestra in order for it to relate to its audience and thereby demonstrate its value to the community. The film's formal elements, including the privileging of Judy's scatting in the frame, emphasize how much more dynamic swing music is than waltzing. In turn, the film shows how much more exciting musical film can be with syncopated forms of music and editing. But lest the waltz be dismissed as outdated, Edna's contributions prove that classical music and swing can coexist and even complement each other; by combining forces, Judy and Edna can appease the fans of each kind of music and demonstrate how a hybridized form only makes them stronger.

During the postwar era, the Hollywood studios released a series of films that increased the level of self-reflexivity that had heretofore structured the genre with more overt commentary on old versus new forms of entertainment. These include *A Song Is Born* (Howard Hawks, 1948; classical versus jazz), *The Barkleys of Broadway* (musical comedy versus legitimate theater), *Singin' in the Rain* (silent cinema versus sound cinema), and *The Band Wagon* (Vincente Minnelli, 1953; musical comedy versus legitimate theater and ballet). In another example from this period, the "Choreography" number in *White Christmas* (Michael Curtiz, 1954), Phil (Danny Kaye) laments the arrival of a new dance form. Flanked by dancers dressed in similarly dark and drab fashion, Phil performs the abrupt and angled movements associated with modern dance, singing, "The theater, the theater / What's happened to the theater? / Especially where dancing is concerned," the lyrics written for the film by Irving Berlin. With the arrival of Judy (Vera Ellen) in a hot-pink, hip-length coat, ruffled bloomers, and high heels, the dancers become transfixed. They watch attentively as she taps with rapid speed, dances in a joyous and presentational fashion, and couples with an equally exciting male partner (John Brascia). Phil attempts to vie for her attention, but ultimately he fails to convert her to his more conceptual style of dancing. At the end of the number, Judy and her partner stand at the center, smiling toward the camera, while Phil and his dancers look on with anguished expressions.

"Choreography" is a comical treatment of the clash between old forms and new. In this case, the "new" is modern dance, ostentatiously referred to, as the song implies, as "choreography" rather than the more colloquial "dance." The number demonstrates how color, swing music, and tap remain as the ultimate purveyors of popular entertainment. Phil and the dancers perform "choreography" with a series of awkward and heavy movements, communicating that modern dance is an intellectual exercise that takes all the fun out of real dancing. And, true to form, the number ends with a vindication of popular dance, the kind that the musical film has embraced since its beginning, symbolized by the coupling of Judy with her jazz-dancing partner.

But rather than being a rejection of old or new forms, most musical films make an idealistic argument for integration and hybridization. As such, they provide audiences with instances in which the genre, and its association with specific forms of song and dance, transforms to adapt to changing times. The popular roller-skating musical *Xanadu* does this perhaps most overtly. In the number "Dancin'," two forms of music, swing and rock, and two historical periods, the 1940s and the 1980s, combine as one. The friends Danny (Gene Kelly) and Sonny (Michael Beck) stand in an empty nightclub and imagine how to revive it. Danny wants "real smooth dances, a wild trombone, the band decked out in tuxedos." The film shows us what he has in mind with a 1940s bandstand, swing dancers, and a female singing group in the image of the Andrews Sisters. In response, Sonny exclaims, "This is the '80s!" In another corner of the nightclub, he conjures "six guys wearing electric orange, a synthesizer, heavy percussion, electric guitar!" The film cuts between both spaces, signaling the differences in style, color, dance, and music between them. Ultimately, however, male-female couples from one dancing group meet one another and exchange partners. In a long shot, we see their respective tiered stages begin to move toward each other and finally integrate together so that they become indistinguishable. The two songs also become intertwined, signaling how they are not so different after all. In the end, Danny's and Sonny's visions are one, and they commit to realizing a revitalized nightclub space that satisfies both of their dreams.

In the twenty-first century, the musical continues to demonstrate the self-referential qualities of pastiche and hybridity. Baz Luhrmann's anachronistic exploration of fin de siècle Paris in *Moulin Rouge* (2001) juxtaposes songs from very different historical moments (like "Nature Boy" from the 1940s) with the world of the cancan, revising what musical film can look and sound like once again. Julie Taymor's *Across the Universe* (2007) also engages in juxtaposition, creating an original story about coming of age in the 1960s and reinterpreting the style and meaning of the Beatles' songbook in the process. Films like *A Prairie Home Companion* (Robert Altman, 2006) and *Mamma Mia* (Phyllida Lloyd, 2008) use musical styles and iconic songs from another era to tell contemporary stories about friendship and family. And, of course, the first iteration of the popular *Step Up* (Anne Fletcher, 2006) franchise brought to the fore once again the presumed conflict between old and new dance styles (ballet versus hip hop) and reconciled them through the integration of the movements, and romantic affections, of a young man and woman.

Both of Damien Chazelle's musicals, *Guy and Madeline on a Park Bench* and *La La Land*, reflect on the future of jazz as a musical style and an art form. Jazz appears to be in crisis in both films, but it is more overtly expressed in *La La Land*, in which Seb laments to Mia outright, "Jazz is dying." He explains, "Everyone says, 'Let it die. It had its time,'" to which he responds, "Well, not on my watch." His purist approach to the art form is placed in harsh relief by his friend Keith (John Legend), who embraces evolution and hybridity in his music; he writes original songs as opposed to reinterpreting old ones and incorporates synthesizer and contemporary performance styles into his shows. Seb's arc as a character depends on his reconciliation of his attitudes about jazz and its future as an evolving art form. With this dialogue at the center of the narrative, *La La Land* is another example of how the musical film continues to grapple with its own cultural origins, educating its audience on where it has been and where it might go in the future. The final scene in the film, which takes place at Seb's newly opened jazz club, indicates that, yes, jazz will continue to live on. And in the process, Chazelle communicates that other cultural forms, like the musical, might just do so as well.

SOLACE

The musical archives itself with the use of multiple self-reflexive devices, including quotation and pastiche and hybridity in order to regenerate anew. It signals its enduring appeal by incorporating the stars and characters of musicals past into its narrative. And it performs its own evolution with the simulation of older musical styles in the present and its explicit juxtaposition and integration of different cultural forms for new audiences. But to what end? To be certain, the musical has been an enduring genre, signaling that its elasticity is one of its most essential qualities. In the late 1960s and 1970s, changing social norms and tastes necessitated that producers infuse their films with social realism, including themes of violence and cruelty, poverty and inequality. The musical adapted accordingly. Bob Fosse's films about the rise of Nazism (*Cabaret*, 1972) and infidelity and death (*All That Jazz*) still evoke the ways that the musical and musical performance can offer solace in a dark world. In *Cabaret*, many of the songs are stark reminders of how we as a society use entertainment in order to distract us from sinister and complex forces ("life is a cabaret, old chum"), but in at least one number, "Maybe This Time," the main character uses the stage to express her hopes for a better future. And in *All That Jazz*, Fosse reveals how the world of Broadway musical comedy is at once a farce ("it's showtime, folks!") but also the protagonist's only way of making sense of his world. As he lies on his hospital deathbed, he imagines his daughter, girlfriend, and ex-wife in a musical number that delineates all the ways he has "gotta change his ways."

Since the turn of the twenty-first century, directors of musical films continue to interpret and apply the genre's historical function of meeting life's challenges. As Richard Dyer notes about the Hollywood musical, the genre offers "temporary answers"—abundance, energy, intensity, transparency, and community—to what we find lacking in society (2002, 22, 26). More recent musicals still provide these temporary answers but in the most extreme of circumstances. Drawing stark comparisons between the more innocent times of musicals past and the horrific realities of the most victimized among us, Lars von Trier quotes *The Sound of Music* (Robert Wise, 1965) repeatedly in his original musical film *Dancer in the Dark* (Lars von Trier, 2000). Throughout the film, Selma (Bjork) allows herself a modicum of happiness by going to the movies to watch musicals like *Forty-Second Street* (Lloyd Bacon, 1933) and by performing in a community production of *The Sound of Music*. As her eyesight fails due to a congenital condition, she loses her part in the play and must settle for listening to musicals rather than watching them. In the pivotal scene at the end when Selma sits in a prison cell waiting to be executed, she begins to sing "My Favorite Things," the song Maria (Julie Andrews) sings to the von Trapp children when they are frightened by a thunderstorm. While von Trier creates a situation that is much more dire than thunder and lightning, he allows the main character nevertheless to find comfort in recalling *The Sound of Music*; with no other accompaniment than the sound of her own voice and physical movements, she finds momentary pleasure in singing and dancing one last time.

Extreme situations inform another twenty-first-century musical, this one made by the Taiwanese film-maker Tsai Ming-liang. In *The Hole* (*Dong*, 1998), "the man upstairs" (Lee Kang-sheng) and "the woman down-stairs" (Yang Kuei-mei) are some of the few to remain in their apartment building despite an apocalyptic sickness that has nearly wiped out the population of the city. Tor-rential rains help the spread of disease, and eventually the woman catches it, causing her to crawl on the floor like a cockroach and seek seclusion in dark spaces. A small hole that exists in the floor of the man's apartment pro-vides a point of contact between them. And while they have annoyed each other for most of the film, he rescues her at the end, pulling her out of her hiding place and into the light of his apartment. Throughout the narrative, however, "the woman downstairs" reimagines her dismal life in a series of musical numbers. She lip-syncs to songs that Grace Chang performed in the 1950s and that recall the singer's roles in Hong Kong musical films (*It Blossoms Again*, 1954; *Mambo Girl*, 1957) of that decade (Ma 2015). Energy, joy, and color infuse the musical numbers that she conjures in moments of despair and exhaustion. Yet they are not wholly separated from her actual life. In one transition, "the woman downstairs" is taking a bath and begins to sneeze, a sign that the sickness is upon her. The film then cuts to her performance of "Achoo Cha Cha," a Grace Chang number about being sick from too much male affection. She dances playfully on a staircase, wearing a sequined dress with pink feathers while flanked by male dancers in suits. Although the numbers sit apart from the narrative in time, they nevertheless reconstitute the space of the apartment building, transforming it from a place of dreariness to playfulness. When "the man upstairs"' ultimately rescues "the woman downstairs," the act leads to the first physical contact between them and manifests itself as a dance. In effect, the world of realism and the world of fantasy merge into one and make possible the characters' communion at the end of the film.

Finally, in the Swedish filmmaker Niki Lindroth von Bahr's animated musical short *Min börda* (*The Burden*, 2017), anthropomorphized fish, mice, monkeys, and dogs reflect the state of humanity and human connection in a world where everyone is alienated and alone. In four segments, von Bahr explores the nighttime world of an office park, hotel, supermarket, and fast-food restaurant. In each location, the animals express feelings of loneliness as a condition of being social outcasts (the fish at the "Long Time Hotel") and of being night-shift workers (the mice, monkeys, and dog) in a space that is entirely shut off from humanity. Once they begin to sing and dance, however, the animals become exuberant and find community with one another. In the second segment, two mice in the fast-food restaurant perform their cleaning duties quietly with only the high-pitched tones of their shoes hitting the tile floor. One begins to turn these sounds into a tap routine, inspiring the other mouse to join him in a number that becomes raucous. They tip over chairs and throw trash into the air. Trays and mops become their props, a form of bricolage that Jane Feuer has identified as being a part of Fred Astaire's and Gene Kelly's ability to effect spontaneity by transforming worldly objects into the realm of fantasy (2002, 33). Von Bahr ends the film with all of the animals lifting their voices, anticipating the moment when there will be "no sorrows, no troubles, when the burden is lifted." But as the film zooms out to view this world from a distance, we see that it is completely isolated, floating atop a massive rock in the middle of a dark universe. The burden may not ever be lifted for these characters, but in the meantime, they find solace, in musical expression and community, when and where they can.

•

Despite the sense of surprise with which journalists and critics repeatedly greet the production of each new musical film, the musical's history has been a story about continuity more than rupture. One of its most fundamental qualities, its function as its own archive, has ensured its continuity with the past of musical film and of musical entertainment. It is a remarkably elastic genre that has shown its ability to remain salient to audiences long after the Hollywood golden age, when it was in the interest of the studios to use the musical as the "quintessential Hollywood product" that contained its own system of advertising in its very structure and perpetuated a "myth of entertainment" that was synonymous with Hollywood itself. Student filmmakers, independent directors, and directors of foreign, art-house cinema have created original works that demonstrate their own personal connection to the genre's history but also apply the genre to contemporary contexts and situations. Reaching back in order to go forward in a continuous circular movement, the history of the musical shows that everything old is new again.

2

THE MUSICAL AS SOCIETY

In 2018, Warner Bros. released the fourth version of *A Star Is Born* (Bradley Cooper, 2018). This latest interpretation tells the story of a female performer, Ally, played by Lady Gaga, who is discovered and delivered to fame by a male rock star, Jack, played by the director Bradley Cooper himself. Their romantic relationship leads to marriage, but it quickly becomes strained; her rising success parallels his increasingly stagnant career. In the end, as with all of the film versions that came before it, the husband commits suicide in the name of no longer being a burden to his wife. He releases her from the responsibility of attending to his many problems. Through it all, the wife proves herself willing to go to great lengths to help him. And in each version's final scene, we find her making a public show, in statement or in song, of her continued devotion to keeping his memory alive.

As the backstage musical developed in Hollywood, it has historically negotiated the relationship between the performers' individual and public selves. The genre straddles onstage spaces of performance, where the public self is manifest, and backstage spaces of reality, where the public self gets revealed as a construction, a mask. As such, the backstage musical has been an opportune cultural text for exploring the lives of people whose social identities are sites of spectacle, performativity, and production.

Women, whose bodies are spectacularized objects in Western culture, have most often been at the center of these stories. There are certainly important exceptions, such as Al Jolson's films (such as *The Jazz Singer*, Alan Crosland, 1927; *The Singing Fool*, Lloyd Bacon, 1928) and the musicals about his life (*The Jolson Story*, Alfred E. Green, 1946; *Jolson Sings Again*, Henry Levin, 1949), but ultimately, the vast number of backstage musicals that have been made are, in essence, stories about women and women's choices. Some of the earliest backstage musicals, *Glorifying the American Girl* (Millard Webb, 1929), *Sally* (John Francis Dillon, 1929), *The Broadway Melody* (Harry Beaumont, 1929), and *Applause* (Rouben Mamoulian, 1929), featured narratives in which women, as individuals, sisters, mothers, and daughters, navigate the pleasures and perils of show-business careers. The genre has continued its focus on women today, as the latest *A Star Is Born* proves.

What is notable about the genre's evolution, however, is that while it has predominantly focused on women, its stories have almost entirely been told by men. To be sure, there were few female directors working in Hollywood during its classical period (1930–60), a condition of the industrial mode of production and the gender exclusivity that it normalized. If we look beyond the classical era and outside Hollywood, we find more women who have participated in this genre. These include Julie Dash's independently produced musical short film *Illusions* (1982), Allison Anders's *Grace of My Heart* (1996), Gina Prince-Bythewood's *Beyond the Lights* (2014), and various films in the *Step Up* (2006–) and *Pitch Perfect* (2015–) franchises. And moving beyond Hollywood and the United States entirely, we see that an array of women filmmakers have taken up the genre to portray complex female characters, including Agnès Varda in France (*Cleo from 5 to 7*, 1962; *One Sings, the Other Doesn't*, 1977), Gillian Armstrong in Australia (*Starstruck*, 1982), Maria Novaro in Mexico (*Danzón*, 1991), and Sally Potter in England/ France/Argentina (*The Tango Lesson*, 1997).

Beyond the relationship between women and the backstage musical, however, we can find multiple instances in which the musical film engages and mediates other societal issues. Inasmuch as the genre concerns itself with social integration and community formation (typically through moments of song and dance), themes of tolerance—toward racial, ethnic, classed, and sexual Others—have been pervasive. Again, we can trace these themes to the beginning of the genre with *The Jazz Singer*, a play and then a film about a Jewish immigrant, written by a Jewish playwright and then produced by a studio founded by four Jewish immigrant brothers, in which the conflict between Jewish filial piety and the seductiveness of American success is overt. Intolerance toward foreigners, outcasts, and people who exist on the margins is an oft-repeated narrative component in musical films, from *South Pacific* (Joshua Logan, 1958) and *The Music Man* (Morton DaCosta, 1962) to *Hairspray* (Adam Shankman, 2007) and *The Greatest Showman* (Michael Gracey, 2017). Most of the films, as with those about women, have been directed by (albeit sympathetic) outsiders to the groups and issues being represented.

This chapter examines the musical's relationship to society and social issues. But it focuses on those backstage musicals that are made by people of color, second-generation immigrants, and women, around whom their narratives of assimilation and cultural resistance, acceptance and rejection, and the possibilities for opportunity and happiness turn. What happens to the musical when a Chicano filmmaker creates a narrative about Mexican American life in Los Angeles? What happens to the musical when a black filmmaker takes on the objectification and spectacularization of the musical black body? And what happens to the musical when a woman director rejects the false dichotomy of love versus career and instead focuses on other aspects of women's relationship to romance and musicality? While these are just a few examples of the much larger body of musical films in existence, they nevertheless help us to understand just how the musical, and the backstage musical in particular, has historically been a pliable tool for acknowledging and mediating issues of social concern and, more importantly, has been an aesthetic language that people on the margins have used to tell their own stories in ways that are often at odds with the norm.

LA BAMBA (LUIS VALDEZ, 1987)

When Luis Valdez's first original musical, *Zoot Suit* (1981), did not recoup Warner Bros.' investment, the playwright and filmmaker set out to prove that he could make a box-office hit. A Mexican American who grew up in a migrant family in Delano, California, Valdez was keenly aware of social inequalities in the United States. He was shamed at school for bringing Mexican food in his lunch box, and he witnessed how his migrant-worker parents struggled to put food on the table for their children. In the 1960s, he joined the United Farm Workers movement and created the Teatro Campesino, the farmworkers' theater, in solidarity with labor activism in the fields. He believed in using song as a form of struggle, and his plays combined music with puppetry and the distancing devices of Brechtian theater in order to portray and publicize why labor organizing was necessary and how it could be achieved.

Valdez's first play-turned-film, *Zoot Suit*, was a period piece set in the years 1942 and 1943, the time of the infamous Sleepy Lagoon murder trial, then the largest mass trial in US history, in which thirteen Mexican American youths were charged for the murder of one boy, and the Zoot Suit Riots, race riots during which American sailors beat Mexican American boys in the streets of Los Angeles. Notably, *Zoot Suit* marked the first time that a major Hollywood studio, Warner Bros., contracted a Mexican American to direct a film. But the studio gave him a paltry budget and a two-week shooting schedule, citing his relative inexperience in the industry. The resulting product is true to its original form as a play at the Mark Taper Forum; it aggressively forces its audience to reckon with the United States' racist past and places at the center of the narrative a controversial figure, the *pachuco*, a zoot-suit-wearing Mexican American man who is prone to violence as a means of survival in a hostile world. The film uses song and dance sequences at once to celebrate the excitement of 1940s nightclubs where Mexican American teenagers spent much of their time and to highlight the racism that led to their mass conviction and imprisonment.

For Valdez's subsequent film, he continued the theme of intolerance toward the Mexican American community, but he did so with a radically different narrative formula. He made a biopic about the life of the 1950s rock 'n' roll star Ritchie Valens. The film follows Ritchie Valenzuela, played by Lou Diamond-Phillips, a young Mexican American boy growing up in Pacoima, California, as he pursues his dream of playing rock 'n' roll, all the while caring for his mother, Connie (Rosanna DeSoto), managing the self-hatred of his half brother, Bob (Esai Morales), and falling in love with a white classmate, Donna (Danielle Von Zerneck).

In many ways, *La Bamba* follows the same rags-to-riches trajectory of other biopics and backstage musicals. Indeed, as Krin Gabbard has observed, the film is effectively a "remake" of *The Jazz Singer*, given that it repeats the theme of retaining one's cultural heritage despite the pressures of assimilation (1996, 60). We first encounter Ritchie working in a migrant camp alongside his mother and younger siblings. Bob has made some money after being released from prison and moves them to a small house that allows them enough stability to attend school regularly. Connie knows that her son has talent and so pulls strings to have Ritchie play a local concert, where a record producer discovers him. Ritchie records and releases songs that become hits, "Well, Let's Go" and "We Belong Together." He begins to play larger concerts and makes enough money to buy a car and a larger home in a nicer area of town for his mother. The film suggests that he would have continued to rise as a rock 'n' roll star were it not for the fact that he died in a plane accident, along with Buddy Holly and J. P. "The Big Bopper" Richardson, after a concert in Clear Lake, Iowa, in 1959.

While the film is ultimately an American success story, cut short only by a freak accident of fate, it nevertheless harbors a trenchant critique of American society. We see the harsh living conditions of the Valenzuela family even after they move out of the labor camp. While the shack that Bob moves them into is better than what they had before, it is dilapidated and in an impoverished section of town. Offering a stark contrast, Valdez takes care to provide a slow tracking shot of Donna's neighborhood, with its new and pristine ranch homes and its lush green lawns.

We also see multiple points of intolerance and discrimination manifested toward Latinos in the 1950s. Donna's father repeatedly thwarts her attempts to spend time with Ritchie. When asked why, he says, "He plays goddamn

cholo music, need I say more?" By identifying Ritchie
with Mexican gang culture, he taps into the same forms
of racism that led to historical injustices like the Sleepy
Lagoon murder trial, acts of violence like the Zoot Suit
Riots, and many others.

Ritchie must confront discrimination in the professional world as well. His manager convinces him to
change his name from Valenzuela to "Valens," a means
of making him more palatable to a broad audience. And
he scoffs when Ritchie suggests a rock 'n' roll version of
the Mexican folk song "La Bamba" for the B-side of his
album: "Rock 'n' roll in Spanish? You gotta be crazy!"
When Ritchie is reminded that he does not speak Spanish, he exclaims, "If Nat King Cole can sing in Spanish, so
can I, right?"

This latter point is an example of how Valdez is able
to complicate the representation of Latinos in his film.
The fact that Ritchie is not bilingual and comes from a
Mexican family suggests that he is an assimilated American. It also points to a specific generational moment in
Mexican American history when the second generation,
the sons and daughters of immigrants, came of age in the
1940s and 1950s, the era of "becoming Mexican American," as the historian George Sánchez has identified it
(1993). They lived bicultural lives but not necessarily
bilingual ones; this was also the generation that suffered

punishment in school for speaking their parents' native tongue. Ritchie's decision to record a song in Spanish indicates a return to his roots. It also marks a pivotal moment in American culture when Spanish entered the mainstream of popular music.

These various themes converge when Ritchie performs "La Bamba" at a rock concert. It is a large theater that is packed with young men and women ready to hear and dance to the music of the rock 'n' roll superstars Chuck Berry and Eddie Cochran. Both of these performers have riled up the audience, performing their iconic songs "Lonely Teardrops" and "Summertime Blues." Ritchie steps out onstage with his guitar, wearing a snakeskin jacket and a talisman from Mexico, a sharp contrast to the more formal dress of the previous performers. The camera cuts to his hand strumming the opening notes on his guitar and pans upward to Ritchie's face as he begins the lyric. The film then cuts to the audience members who have instantly jumped to their feet. For the duration of the number, the audience expresses its approval by cheering, clapping, and dancing to the song. Valdez privileges the audience in this sequence, devoting the majority of the shots to framing the audience either by themselves or with Ritchie in the back- or foreground. Certainly, the audience's reaction communicates Ritchie's success in this moment. But, more importantly, the multiple shots of the audience allow Valdez to demonstrate the cultural hybridity that makes up US society, as reflected by the audience's interracial and multiethnic demographics and their reaction to a hybridized form of music, Mexican folk and American rock 'n' roll. With the reaction to "La Bamba," Valdez is able to demonstrate the contributions that Mexicans have made to American music. And by foregrounding the multiracial and multicultural dimensions of this one moment, Valdez can show how the potential for a new United States is being born.

Like *Zoot Suit* before it, *La Bamba* takes a critical stance toward US society. Though not as strident in its mode of delivery, Valdez's later film is perhaps more effective in its message given that its cinematic language and familiar narrative structure allowed it to reach more people. The soundtrack album went platinum twice just two months after the film's release. And with the added support of Latinos who saw the film in US Spanish-language theaters, where the film had been Spanish dubbed or Spanish subtitled by Columbia Pictures, it grossed $5.6 million domestically. At least at the time, the film's radical revisioning of Latinos in film, and the kinds of films that can tell stories about Latino lives, seemed to play out at the box office. The *Los Angeles Times* writer Victor Valle noted how *La Bamba* forced industry executives to acknowledge the power of the Latino market and to recognize that, despite decades of Hollywood imagery, Latinos desired more than just "films with hefty doses of sex and violence" (1987).

BAMBOOZLED (SPIKE LEE, 2000)

A satire about race, representation, and the modern media, Spike Lee's *Bamboozled* (2000) remains a provocative work of filmmaking. The plot centers on the production of a musical variety program for television, a "new millennium minstrel show" with blackface performers and comedy skits. Its chief author, Pierre Delacroix (Damon Wayans), intends for it to fail immediately, thereby liberating him from his job at a failing television network. But to his surprise, the show is an instant hit. It quickly overcomes concerns regarding political correctness and sparks a blackface craze across the nation.

As a film about the making of a musical show, *Bamboozled* falls squarely within the backstage musical tradition. In that genre, the characters move from distinct offstage and backstage spaces to onstage ones. Their identities shift accordingly from their "real" and private selves to their stage personas or public selves. And musical sequences, including both song and dance numbers, are contained by the parameters of the stage and occasionally a rehearsal hall.

Central to the backstage musical's structure and thematics is the existence of the audience within the diegetic world of the film. As Jane Feuer has theorized, "before television invented the studio audience and canned laughter, the Hollywood musical was putting audiences into the film for the purpose of shaping the responses of the movie audience to the film" (1982, 26). This audience within the film could instruct the audience of the film itself on how to receive the entertainment being provided onscreen. With few exceptions, the audience within the film greeted the entertainment with unequivocal approbation.

The second function of the built-in audience, Feuer has observed, is its ability to simulate the experience of live performance (1982, 26). If the film's audience can be made to identify with the fictional audience inside the film, then the film becomes all the more convincing as entertainment. The performance being given therefore takes on qualities of vitality and dynamism and overcomes the fact that it is only "canned" entertainment in the process.

Bamboozled places both of these functions of the audience in backstage musicals into harsh relief. Lee's built-in audience is the one inside the television studio where Delacroix shoots the "new millennium minstrel show." The minstrel-show audience is indeed a barometer for how well the show is doing in the minds of the film's audience. And with frequent shots of their "real-time" reactions, Lee gives the film's audience an experience of being there.

Bamboozled departs from the formula, however, in the nature of the relationship between the "show," its built-in audience, and its actual audience. Whereas the audiences in Hollywood musicals of an earlier era almost always gave their approval for a performance, this same convention in Lee's film produces troubling results. Taking on the history of black representation in mainstream US culture, Lee sets out to make the subject of looking at and spectacularizing black people as his central point of critique.

It is significant to note that there have been very few backstage musicals that feature black American characters as anything other than the servants of the film's white stars or as performers who are restricted to their onstage song and dance numbers and have little to nothing to do with the film's plot. If the purpose of many of these backstage musicals is to chart the possibilities for romance and social mobility for the main character, and twentieth-century racial logics precluded black Americans from participating in such opportunities, then it stands to reason why they would be excluded from the film's narrative in this way. As one-off performers, like the Nicholas

Brothers (Fayard and Harold Nicholas) in *Down Argentine Way* (Irving Cummings, 1940), for example, the tap-dancing duo could be featured as an engaging source of entertainment and simultaneously denied integration into the film's larger plot about traveling to exotic locations and the pursuit of romantic relationships. As Sean Griffin (2002) has noted regarding the 20th Century Fox musicals in particular, there are ways that such segregated performances provided the artists with greater control over their appearances and representation. Nevertheless, the musical treated them merely as "musical props," to use the filmmaker Julie Dash's line from *Illusions*, her own film about black Americans in Hollywood musicals of the 1940s. And, as Miriam J. Petty (2016) has shown, if black performers, from their highly circumscribed position, exhibited talent that was too exceptional, they could be accused of "stealing the show" from the white stars who surrounded them. Such was the case with the singer and dancer Jeni LeGon, whom MGM repeatedly denied roles, despite her contract with the studio, precisely because she might upstage her adjacent performers.

Exceptions to black performance in backstage musicals include films that were limited in other ways. The Hollywood studios allowed black performers to be featured as characters who rise up the social ladder through show business in films where black characters played every role. These all-black-cast musicals, like *Stormy Weather* (Andrew L. Stone, 1943), existed in a hermetically sealed social world in which overt forms and residual effects of structural racism do not exist. And in "race movies," films made by and for black audiences, like *The Duke Is Tops* (Ralph Cooper, 1938), producers could more fully explore depictions of black romance and social mobility, but these too existed in a parallel entertainment landscape to the more dominant and more prevalent Hollywood cinema.

Spike Lee upends these traditions of racial representation as they have been handed down through commercial cinema. He places black characters at the center of the story, and they occupy both backstage and onstage space, plot, and performance. Accordingly, they enjoy the benefits of social mobility as a result of their stage work. The featured characters in the minstrel show, Savion Glover as "Mantan" and Tommy Davidson as "Sleep 'n' Eat," go from being members of New York's homeless population to living in furnished, skyrise apartments as a result of the show's success. And yet, rather than providing the happy ending that characterized other backstage musicals, the success of the show is discomfiting, and it represents the worst rather than the best of US society. Rather than entertaining us with virtuosic performances (like the Nicholas Brothers and so many other black entertainers have done in such films), Mantan and Sleep 'n' Eat shock and appall us.

Lee consistently pulls the film's audience out of their complacent position as spectators and forces them to reckon with their relationship to the entertainment being given. This occurs on two levels, both of which involve the audiences inside and outside the film. In the first, Lee exploits the relationship between the audience in the television studio and the one that is watching his film. We see this from the first time the minstrel show begins filming. As Mantan and Sleep 'n' Eat enter the stage via a giant mouth of a caricatured blackface figure, shots of the audience, which Lee takes care to distinguish as a demographically heterogeneous group, expose their skeptical and offended faces. After the performers finish a comedy sketch, Mantan begins a tap number and is joined by fellow dancers in pickaninny, mammy, jungle savage, and Uncle Tom costumes. Shots of the audience reveal that some of them are beginning to laugh and clap. As the number continues, the tap dancers win them over. We see a white male audience member glance around to see if others are cheering, and being sufficiently satisfied that it is socially acceptable to applaud, he joins in. The number ends with a close-up of Mantan's face in a smiling grimace. Beads of sweat saturate his blackface makeup, which the television studio's bright lights emphasize.

Initially, we encounter an audience that we can identify with. Just like them, we are horrified by the show. But as the number continues, the diegetic audience begins to shift away from our position. In the process, we, the film's audience, realize we can no longer be guided by the audience we see on the screen. To emphasize the point, the close-up of Mantan's grotesque blackface mask makes us aware of the act of looking; Lee forces us to readjust and reassess this spectatorial position as a result.

The act of looking takes on a different dimension as Lee shifts modes in the film, embedding documentary film within the fictional narrative at multiple points. He injects the documentary form into *Bamboozled* at precise moments to educate the characters onscreen and the film's audience about the history of black performance and blackface minstrelsy in particular. Before the sequence just described, for example, we see the characters in their respective dressing rooms getting ready for the performance. The scene begins with Sloan (Jada Pinkett Smith), Pierre's assistant, giving voice-over narration as Mantan and Sleep 'n' Eat "black up": "As usual I did my research: . . . pour alcohol on cork, burn to a crisp, mash to a powder, add water." We see the characters follow her disembodied instruction and then begin to apply the burnt cork to their faces. In other moments, she instructs onscreen, as when she gives Pierre a "jolly n—— bank," a black collectible figurine from the turn of the century that rolls its eyes when Pierre drops a penny into its mouth. She explains, "It reminds me of a time in our history when we were considered inferior, subhuman, and we should never forget." Like the end of the minstrel-show number, Lee ends this sequence with an extreme close-up of the figurine's shiny and distorted face. Sloan's function is to narrate and instruct for the benefit of the film's audience. In turn, we are made aware of ourselves as being spoken to. Our position is a dynamic one rather than passive.

The film ventures in and out of the documentary mode but ultimately settles there at the end. Lee provides a montage of footage, from silent cinema to classical Hollywood cinema to animated cartoons. It is a barrage of derogatory images that evoke the many ways that mainstream media has stereotyped black Americans. The repetition of black stereotypes—happy-go-lucky, lazy, watermelon and chicken eating, savages—and the white stars who have appropriated them, from Al Jolson and Bing Crosby to Judy Garland and Shirley Temple, reveals just how imbricated notions of black inferiority have been in our popular consciousness.

Moreover, the majority of the images in the montage are of singing and dancing black bodies, troubling our understanding of our entertainment heritage and the musical in particular. Lee's own reliance on song and dance sequences for the minstrel show reproduces this history for a millennium audience. In his hands, the backstage musical is not a celebration of entertainment. Rather, *Bamboozled* uses the cinematic language of the musical, the genre's tools of the built-in audience and racial spectacle in particular, to interrogate the genre as a whole as a product built on the notion of black inferiority and primitivism.

THE TANGO LESSON (SALLY POTTER, 1997)

Toward the end of Julie Dash's *Illusions*, a film set in 1940s Hollywood, the female movie producer Ms. Dupree explains why she entered the industry. "I wanted to take charge of the motion picture," she says, "because there are many stories to be told and many battles to begin." Dash's film repeatedly reflects on the influential power of Hollywood to create illusions that are taken as truths. One central illusion is the construction of women as idealized objects. The film refers to multiple forms of illusion, including racialized and gendered ones in the industry. Ms. Dupree's final words express Dash's own project of telling new stories and fighting old ones as someone whose identity, being black and being a woman, has historically been shut out of positions of influence in Hollywood.

Tellingly, the main character's job in *Illusions* is to make musicals, which, as we witness in the film, features a white woman singing and dancing. But her voice is not her own; it belongs to a young black woman who will not be credited in the final product. In one shot in particular, these power dynamics come into focus. In a darkened studio soundstage, we see the singer in long shot at the left of the frame as she watches a large screen on which the white star performs the number. Between them sits the reflection of a male sound engineer who is charged with creating the final illusion of white female perfection. As Dash demonstrates, the musical is especially invested in the performance of femininity, but it has almost always been at the direction of men who sit at the controls. As Ms. Dupree explains, if things "don't change in this industry, then they aren't going to change at all."

A limited number of female filmmakers, most of them working outside the United States, have taken up the call to change the script regarding the relationship among femininity, performance, and the musical film. Some of these reflect on the definition of womanhood itself, focusing on how women experience the tension between objectification and subjectivity (*Dance, Girl Dance*, Dorothy Arzner, 1940; *Cléo from 5 to 7*; *Danzón*; *Beyond the Lights*). Many of these films foreground female homosocial and familial relationships over heterosexual romance (*One Sings, the Other Doesn't; Starstruck; Danzón*). Some even go so far as to portray female characters who are content to be without a male partner in the end (*Dance, Girl Dance; One Sings, the Other Doesn't; Illusions; Starstruck; Danzón; Grace of My Heart*).

The Tango Lesson, Sally Potter's pseudoautobiographical film about a female director who learns tango and sets out to make a movie about it, grapples with all of these issues. It is decidedly against the grain of the Hollywood film-musical tradition in that it privileges female agency and desire over male control and authorship. At the start of the film, Sally already has achieved success in her career, and she seeks out the tango as a means of self-fulfillment rather than a means of survival. But she does not deny herself the romance, and even vulnerability, that the tango provides at the hands of her costar and choreographer, Pablo Verón, who plays himself. The film, which is structured according "lessons," is as much an education in the tango as it is an exploration of what it means to be an independent woman who feels the need, at different times, to both lead and follow.

The film communicates this best in two scenes that involve musical performance. In the first, Sally and Pablo celebrate the first night of Hanukkah in his apartment. While she lights the candles at the dining table, he cooks dinner in the adjacent kitchen. She suggests that she might scrap her current film project in order to make a movie about the tango, which, as she explains, would be "something that is more myself." Pablo glances at her with surprise and then, pleased with the idea, returns to the preparation of the meal. He punctuates his activity by twirling a napkin between his hands and then leaping over it, making a loud stamp with his feet. The sound initiates a dance sequence for which he employs the accoutrement of the kitchen—the towel, a hanging sheet of foil, pots, and pans—recalling the "bricolage" numbers crafted by Fred Astaire and Gene Kelly before him (Feuer 1982). Like those earlier musical film stars, Pablo uses his hands and his feet to create a syncopated rhythm that functions as music. And he keeps his eyes on Sally, signaling that he hopes to entertain and impress her with each new surprising move.

In addition to demonstrating that Verón is an accomplished tap dancer as well as tango dancer, the scene is one of seduction. And Sally is willing to let it be so. As Pablo dances in the kitchen, he is framed by the doorway that separates their respective positions. Sally watches through this doorway, which functions as a frame within the frame of the film, mesmerized by the spectacle. The long shot that captures his dancing body through the doorway is Sally's point of view, Potter is clear to point out. A cut to the camera's close-up of his feet slowly pans up his body. The film then cuts to a close-up of Sally, who gazes at him with adoration while holding her head in her hands. This pattern in which a long shot of his body is met with a close-up of her act of watching makes clear that it is her desire that is being met here. Whereas earlier Hollywood musicals, and indeed most of Hollywood classical cinema, objectified the female body (often with an upward pan) for the purposes of satisfying male pleasure, Potter appropriates the gaze in this moment (Mulvey 1975). His dancing body has become the object of desire and, she is in control of its power.

The Tango Lesson does not make these revisions to past formulas absolute, however. Pablo enacts the fantasy for Sally, eventually bursting out of the kitchen and onto the fireplace mantel, where he is visually framed once again, this time by the large mirror behind him. Now there are two of him, the real and the virtual. Hinting that part of this seduction might be based on fantasy alone, Potter ends the number abruptly. Pablo jumps down and invites her to dance with him at an upcoming performance. She greets the invitation happily; but almost simultaneously, his telephone rings, and he goes to answer it. The spell is broken as she turns from him and slowly walks out of the frame.

Just as strongly as Potter redirects the gaze and reverses the gendered orientation of subject and object, so too does she emphasize the complexity of relationships that are built on idealisms such as those that the musical constructs. We see these fissures more directly in a subsequent scene involving the performance that Pablo and Sally give. The sequence begins as the two dancers emerge from their dressing room, hand in hand, with looks of happy expectation on their faces. The camera provides a medium following shot of the two as they walk quickly through the narrow passageways and winding staircases of the backstage space. They eventually make it to the stage and give each other one last reassuring glance before stepping in front of the audience. Rather than seeing the dancers as the diegetic audience does, however, we remain in an anterior position as spectators. Potter's camera sits upstage looking toward the theater audience with the dancers in the middle ground, silhouetted by the strong spotlight shining down on them from the balcony. The spotlight not only silhouettes the dancers but also obscures the faces of the audience. We see that audience only in extreme long shot as we focus on the dancers' full frames moving across the stage. Such framing precludes the film audience from critical information about the performance being given and the emotions of the performers themselves. Without the visual cues of audience response, we are left in an ambiguous position regarding our relationship to the dance and its role in the film itself.

With one brief exception, Potter prevents us from sharing the audience's position, constraining us to the back edges of the stage instead.

The exceptional moment to this framing occurs toward the end of the number when, abruptly, the camera reverses position and shows the dancers from the audience's point of view. The action is in slow motion as Pablo and Sally perform a lift, but it lasts less than a second, after which we are immediately positioned behind them once again. The front-facing shot functions within the larger number as an indication, however brief, that the dancers are performing their steps successfully; and at the conclusion of the number, we can hear the audience's exuberant applause. But as the characters glance at each other while taking their bows, it becomes clear that something is wrong.

Potter again moves away from the formula of other backstage musicals here. Not only does she deny us the signaling devices that we have come to depend on when a man and a woman take the stage, but she also does not allow for the creation of utopia in performance. Historically, song and dance sequences have provided feelings of elation and liberation and symbolized the romantic union of the male-female couple (Altman 1987). Musicals like *Babes in Arms* (Busby Berkeley, 1939), *Summer Stock* (Charles Walters, 1950); *Dirty Dancing* (Emile Ardolino,

1987), and *Strictly Ballroom* (Baz Luhrmann, 1992) adhere to these functions of the genre. Sally and Pablo's performance, by contrast, produces discomfort for both the characters and the film's audience. And instead of symbolizing union, the dance leads to separation. Given that the couple's big performance number occurs midway through the film rather than at the end signals that the performance will not serve its traditional function as a happy ending.

As Sally and Pablo exit the stage and return to their dressing room, their disunion is clear. They do not hold hands. Instead, Pablo rushes ahead of Sally. She chases after him, asking for his thoughts. Once in the dressing room, they sit at their respective stations at a long, shared table. He proceeds to yell at her and pound his fist: "You should do nothing when you dance, except follow! FOLLOW! Otherwise you block my freedom to move. You destroy my liberty. And then I cannot dance. I cannot dance. I can do nothing." Potter has Pablo deliver this speech in extreme close-up, with his right-side profile at the far left of the frame. Deeply in the background, Sally's body appears small as she buries her face in the table. Their conversation continues while Pablo's face and words visually and figuratively overwhelm Sally's figure. His presence is oppressive, a far cry from the genial and alluring figure he has been previously.

What becomes clear is that Sally has been too "strong" onstage, prompting Pablo to have feelings of masculine insecurity. Sally's relative strength and Pablo's desire to be dominant represent the key tension in their relationship. At times, she acquiesces, but when she does not, they inevitably fall into conflict. Sally says this directly: "It doesn't suit me to follow. It suits me to lead, and you can't deal with that." This tension carries to the end as she makes a film, presumably a musical, given its tango sequences. While Pablo wants to work in film, he resists her position as both lover and director. He complains about her professional behavior: "You have become a camera." As she positioned herself earlier in the film, as the holder of the gaze, she insists, "That's how I love you, with my eyes, with my work."

The Tango Lesson revises how we think about men, women, and the musical. Potter's approach to the musical formula is to acknowledge its seductive powers but to reflect, in a self-reflexive manner, how the formula must shift if a woman holds the camera and writes the story. Romance and fantasy continue to play a role. Indeed, the film ends with Sally and Pablo joyously dancing the tango on the street. But the struggles that have characterized their relationship up to that point qualify an obvious happy ending. Potter leaves us wondering if they will live happily ever after. In this way, Sally's description of her own tango musical applies to Potter's film as a whole. Pablo asks her how many musical numbers there will be. She replies, "It's not a matter of numbers, but there will be a story." *The Tango Lesson* does not subscribe to any strict formulas for the musical. Instead, it offers an exploratory process for what a musical about relationships and the love of dance can be.

•

Using different modes of production and narrative structures, the films discussed here show a full range of how musicals address society. Their creation by members of marginalized and disempowered groups makes them especially significant to the history of how the musical has been told. Through them, we understand how the musical is a genre that has both advanced ethnic and racial stereotype and made issues of intolerance a central concern. The filmmakers Luis Valdez, working albeit tenuously from within Hollywood, and Spike Lee, working through his own independent production company, use their respective films to address both of these interests in the genre. *La Bamba* revises historical representations of Latinos and Mexicans in particular by depicting characters who have complex histories and relationships with their cultural heritage. *Bamboozled* reproduces the stereotype as a means of educating its audience about the sinister powers of racial spectacle. And *The Tango Lesson* treats male-female romance and its musical expression, a central feature of the musical's enduring appeal, as something to be questioned rather than accepted.

Using the convention of the audience within the film is one way that these Latino, black, and female directors have made their revisions to the genre plain. Valdez promotes an identification with the audience, but he does so only by revising what that audience looks like, thereby envisioning a society that embraces rather than disavows this nation's multiethnic and multiracial identity. Lee, by contrast, distances us from the audience for the "new millennium minstrel show," thereby forcing our recognition of pervasive forms of racism. And Potter denies us the audience altogether, setting us adrift when it comes to understanding what performance means in a genre that has attached such symbolic weight to it. As these examples show, the musical is a pliant cinematic language. It spans across a variety of genres (biopics, backstage musicals, back-studio pictures) and accommodates a heterogeneous group of filmmakers who have harnessed its language in the fight for representation and acceptance.

3

THE MUSICAL AS MEDIATION

There is a scene in John Carney's *Begin Again* (2013) that self-consciously employs the tools of cinematic illusion. Dan (Mark Ruffalo), a washed-up talent scout and record producer, stumbles into a New York City bar. He is quickly distracted by the woman playing her guitar and singing on the stage. While Gretta (Keira Knightley) performs, Dan starts to hear and see the abandoned instruments that surround her come alive. One by one, the drums, the strings, and the keyboard accompany her to produce a rich and full sound that complements her simple delivery of the song. As she finishes, the audience, largely unimpressed, reluctantly applauds. But having had a privileged experience, Dan and the film's audience realize the singer's potential. He is the only one to enthusiastically applaud as she exits the stage.

The movie magic in this scene has the potential to lead to another moment of discovery. As Gretta dejectedly slumps down into a couch, Dan sits in front of her, hands

79

her his business card, and announces, "I'm in. I wanna make records with you. I wanna produce you. I wanna sign you. We were meant to work together." He proceeds to tell her how he will make her songs hits and that she is beautiful. Rejecting his assessment of her qualities, which have as much to do with her songwriting as her looks, she states, "I'm not Judy Garland just off a Greyhound bus looking for stardom." She thanks him and returns the card to his shirt pocket. Calling her bluff, Dan walks out of the bar, leaving Gretta alone on the couch.

Like a similar scene in the 1954 version of *A Star Is Born*, in which Judy Garland stars, the one in *Begin Again* involves an older man discovering a younger female talent. He is a drunk and past his prime, while she is vibrant and full of promise. Yet, due to his age and experience, he is in a position to offer her the promise of stardom.

Contrary to *A Star Is Born* (and each of its Hollywood incarnations in 1937, 1954, and 1976), Gretta does not accept Dan's terms for success. She rejects his objectification of her ("I actually just think that music is about ears, not eyes"). And she sends him away rather than being swept up by the opportunity that he represents. While Dan's inebriated state and his initial overconfidence align him with the male protagonist of *A Star Is Born*, he later tells her the truth: he was fired from his job at the record label and is nearly homeless. If she agrees to work with him, it will be for the experience of it, for the love of the music, and as a "tribute to this beautiful, God-damned, crazy, fractured mess of a city, New York." They make an album not within the commercial world of popular entertainment but outside it, with amateur musicians who bring their own instruments and tools to record their music against a backdrop of dynamic urban spaces.

In this way, *Begin Again* signals its departure from musicals that have come before. Gretta is not Judy Garland, and *Begin Again* is not *A Star Is Born*. Rather, this independently produced musical film, Carney's second in a trilogy that includes the Irish musicals *Once* (2007) and *Sing Street* (2016), rewrites the genre's conventions in ways that experience music differently by showing how people create it, play it, and listen to it. These encounters with music take precedent over the genre's more common investment: interweaving the narrative trajectories of putting on a show and finding romance, or the musical's "dual focus narrative," as Rick Altman (1987) has identified it.

By contrast, male-female relations are ambiguous in Carney's musicals. At the end of his films, we are left with more questions than answers about these relationships. Nor does a triumphant show overcome or reconcile the differences between romantic couples. Indeed, in *Begin Again*, the singular moment of a successful performance that would typically signal male-female reunion achieves the exact opposite. It propels the protagonists further from each other. Finally, while music and performance provide the means by which characters can come together, communion happens via the combining of individual talents in an ongoing process of collaboration. There is no entertainment as such because there is no hierarchy between performer and audience. Listening to, creating, and playing music, Carney demonstrates, are transcendent and joyful experiences in their own right.

Carney's work diverges from the Hollywood musical in another critical way. Music is a fundamental mode of communication in his films. In other words, it is not a vehicle for establishing individual distinction and stardom, as in most backstage musicals about putting on a show. Nor does it promise to easily fix social problems like intolerance (*The Greatest Showman*, Michael Gracey, 2017) or racism (*Hairspray*, Adam Shankman, 2007) by overcoming personal differences. Instead, the films *Once*, *Begin Again*, and *Sing Street* foreground music as a form of mediation in order to foster everyday human connection. And it is the materiality of music, its tools, equipment, and devices, that provides the means by which humans encounter one another. Mediating devices abound in Carney's films, including microphones, amps, speakers, Walkmans, Discmans, headphones, headphone splitters,

cassette tapes and cassette players, LPs and record players, smartphones, laptops, and music videos. The types
of recording media that appear range from print media
(written lyrics on a piece of paper) to magnetic tape
inside cassettes to the optical discs of DVDs and to the
smartphone microphones that convert audio signals into
digital ones. In *Sing Street* in particular, it is broadcast
media in the form of music videos that constitute the primary form of expression.

These mediating devices provide the source of the
music onscreen. They answer the ever-present question
asked of the musical, Where does the music come from?
As Carney himself said regarding *Once*, "a modern audience won't get past the fact that people are breaking into
song walking down the street unless the film is very . . .
self-consciously made" (quoted in Fee 2010, 179). But
musical objects also mediate the relationships between
characters and between characters and their environ-
ment. Rather than accepting arguments about how
media and technology atomize society, Carney insists
they bring us together.

Other genres have received more attention for their
relationship to media and forms of mediation. Melo-
dramas like *Rebel without a Cause* (Nicholas Ray, 1955)
and *All That Heaven Allows* (Douglas Sirk, 1955) are notable for their placement of the television set in domestic

living rooms, symbolizing the felt effects of distortion and alienation among family members (Joyrich 1988). In an essay on zombie films, Allan Cameron argues that while science fiction has a "tendency to frame media, and the failure of media, in social terms," using "cutting-edge or speculative technologies," zombie films "place all media under suspicion" (2012, 68). While less studied in this regard, musicals have shown a persistent commitment to reflecting on various forms of media and their dissemination. But instead of being fearful or suspicious of media, the musical embraces and harnesses media's potential for the genre's broader project of creating connection and continuity.

This chapter examines the musical's various forms of mediation. First and foremost, the genre has self-consciously presented itself as a mediated cultural product by referencing the tools of its own production. We see this in the earliest musical films, as well as in scenes in Carney's work like the one this chapter opens with. But musicals have also directly reflected on specific forms of media and technology and how they contribute to the creation of community. Looking outside Hollywood is beneficial here since it is in John Carney's musical films that media and mediation are wedded in a most integral fashion. Each of his films, from *Once* to *Begin Again* to *Sing Street*, foregrounds music as a mediating device that links people together and to the world around them. After an analysis of the Hollywood musical's engagement with mediated forms, this chapter will focus on the three central activities explored in Carney's films: listening to, creating, and playing music. In each, I will demonstrate how his musicals alter the genre's conventions, shifting it away from the celebration of entertainment and toward a thematics of mediated communion.

MUSICALS ON MUSICALS, MEDIA, AND TECHNOLOGY

From the outset, the musical film has had to reckon with its relationship to modern technology. With the birth of the genre upon the coming of sound in the late 1920s, the inclusion of song and dance sequences were one way that studios overcame the problems of exporting their films. Seeking to retain the international dominance that they had achieved as a result of the closure of European production houses during World War I, the Hollywood studios favored musical sequences not only because they featured the new sound technology but also because they did not require dubbing or translation in foreign markets. The sequences were presentational in orientation, often with singers using direct address to the camera, and so facilitated a connection between performer and audience that dialogue sequences did not.

But these same strengths about the genre were also its weakness, especially among contemporary critics. As Charles O'Brien has argued, the disruption of the film's narrative caused by musical numbers appeared to contemporary observers as an atrophying of the form. "Negative critical reaction influenced cinema history for decades afterward," he writes, "as the musical films of the late 1920s and early 1930s were either dismissed as bad cinema or ignored altogether" (2019, 2). Musical films inhibited the advancement of cinema, they insisted, and signaled its adherence to the market rather than the aesthetic heights achieved by silent film.

Not surprisingly, early movie musicals internalized this guilt and integrated discussions of new media and technology into their narrative and formal language. There exists a self-conscious mode in such films in which their problematic relationship to the coming of sound cinema must be declared, neutralized, and integrated into the genre's project of creating community. In *Footlight Parade* (Lloyd Bacon, 1933), for example, the film opens with a shot of a news ticker that scrolls on top of a building: "MOTION PICTURE PRODUCERS ANNOUNCE ONLY TALKING PICTURES WILL BE MADE IN FUTURE—SILENT PICTURES ARE FINISHED." Right away, we understand that the coming of sound cinema threatens to put a hardworking community of Broadway singers, dancers, and producers out of work. No one wants live entertainment anymore. As the director Chester Kent (James Cagney) declares, "Bread line, I hear you calling me." But he soon seizes on an opportunity to produce "prologues," short, live entertainment acts that fill the space between films at the movie theater. Applying a "chain store" model to the production, Chester sustains the tradition of live entertainment, thereby keeping everyone employed, by mass producing the prologues, which allows him to keep costs down. In the end, the performers are happy to keep their jobs, and the joint efforts of Chester and his assistant, Nan Prescott (Joan Blondell), lead them to realize their love for each other. The final scene cuts to black as the lovers kiss and plan for their wedding.

It is the nuclear family and the small-town community that are threatened by sound cinema in *Babes in Arms* (Busby Berkeley, 1939). The vaudeville performer and father Joe Moran (Charles Winninger) is out of work along with his fellow vaudevillians. After a montage sequence in which we see Moran rise to the top of the profession, we read a series of *Variety* headlines: "TALKIES ARRIVE!," "FILM SONGS SWEEP NATION," "GARBO TALKS!," "TALKIES TOP VAUDEVILLE!," and "VAUDEVILLE DOOMED!" During shots of the first two headlines, iris effects open in the middle of the frame to feature scenes from the earliest Hollywood musicals, *The Broadway Melody* (Harry Beaumont, 1929) and *The Hollywood Revue of 1929* (Charles Reisner, 1929). Self-consciously, *Babes in Arms* declares that musical films have caused the demise of family-oriented live entertainment traditions. As a result, the parents decide to leave town to put on a new show, leaving their children behind. While they are away, a meddlesome moral reformer, Martha Steele (Margaret Hamilton), threatens to send the children to state work schools, thereby separating them from their parents for good. Left to defend themselves, the kids put on their own show, led by Moran's son, Mickey (Mickey Rooney), and Patsy Barton (Judy Garland). A variety revue, their production proves that the kids have talent and makes it clear that live performance is still a viable form of entertainment. Their show is such a success that Broadway producers give them a contract that allows them to bring their parents with them. Even though sound cinema has caused significant damage, musical films, *Babes in Arms* implicitly demonstrates, are a force for good in society by keeping family-oriented entertainment traditions alive.

Finally, *Singin' in the Rain* (Stanley Donen and Gene Kelly, 1952) provides an even stronger justification of the musical. "We'll make a musical," declares Kathy Seldon (Debbie Reynolds) when the coming of sound has produced chaos at the fictional Hollywood studio Monumental Pictures. Having tried their hand at making a "talkie" and failed, Don Lockwood (Gene Kelly) and Cosmo Brown (Donald O'Connor) stay up all night feeling dejected about the future of their careers. Don is a swashbuckling silent-film star, akin to Douglas Fairbanks, and Cosmo is an on-set piano accompanist. When Kathy offers her idea, they both demonstrate their abilities to sing and dance and sweep up Kathy in the number "Good Mornin'." Instantly, the invocation of a musical leads to feelings of joy and a sense of camaraderie.

Unlike *Footlight Parade* and *Babes in Arms, Singin' in the Rain* engages with the materiality of the coming of sound. In the scene in which the stars do their first on-set recording, the microphones, wires, sound booth, and recording equipment intrude on the performance. They are awkward additions to the set and cause much distress and confusion. Lina Lamont (Jean Hagen), the star of the film, must have a large and bulky microphone placed inside her costume. Lina cannot adjust her acting to the placement of the mic and must have it repositioned multiple times. The director of the film becomes increasingly frustrated with his lack of control and the necessity of shooting the scene over and over again. And the shoot comes to halt when the producer enters, naively pulls at some wires on the floor, and literally upends Lina, to whom they are attached. The sequence is a comedic one that gently critiques the studios' quick embrace of sound technology many decades earlier. The sound film eventually gets made, but technology fails once again during its first projection in the movie theater. But ultimately, *Singin' in the Rain* conveys that while sound cinema can be difficult, musicals are not. Despite the false starts, the movie that is made within *Singin' in the Rain* and that saves sound cinema from failure is another musical, called *The Dancing Cavalier.*

Makers of musical films employ the technologies that make the genre possible, cinematography, sound recording, and audiovisual projection, in the service of justifying its replacement of silent cinema and its distinctiveness from other forms. In *Footlight Parade* and *Babes in Arms,* it is the musical film's ability to preserve and sustain live entertainment forms that renders its value. And in *Singin' in the Rain,* it is the musical film's ability to save sound cinema that communicates its cultural worth and ensures its popularity into the future.

Beyond incorporating the genesis of sound cinema and musical film into the narrative, there are numerous musicals that reference and incorporate other forms of media. Just as the musical exhibits self-consciousness regarding its role in the coming of sound cinema, so too does it express an insecurity about other mediating forms. In *Rebecca of Sunnybrook Farm* (Allan Dwan, 1938), for example, Aunt Miranda (Helen Westley) prevents her young niece Rebecca Winstead (Shirley Temple) from performing on the radio. Biased against "show people," Aunt Miranda insists that Rebecca spend her childhood away from the city and on the family farm. The experience of country life, with its emphasis on production, stability, and daily routine, seems starkly at odds with the more frantic and consumer-oriented world of the city. To accommodate Rebecca's wish to sing and the producer Anthony Kent's (Randolph Scott) need to find a new voice for his radio show, the radio studio comes to the farm. Kent sets up a recording space in his country home next to Rebecca's where she can easily enjoy both worlds at once, her family and show business. As the voice of the show's sponsor, the cereal Crackly Grain Flakes, Rebecca demonstrates that wholesomeness and consumerism go hand in hand. And *Rebecca of Sunnybrook Farm* reveals how radio is in service to the musical's project of assuaging tensions between family togetherness and the pressures of work.

By midcentury, television threatened the movies just as sound cinema had threatened silent film before it. Musicals attenuated this new form of media as a threat again by demonstrating how family and community could be sustained in the production and dissemination of television shows. In the process, musicals like *My Blue Heaven* (Harry Koster, 1950) and *White Christmas* (Michael Curtiz, 1954) also convey that the musical can incorporate and benefit from television itself. In the former, a married song-and-dance team produces variety acts for television. Kitty (Betty Grable) and Jack (Dan Dailey) Moran enjoy their work and the stability that the television studio provides. Unlike theater performers, they do not live an itinerant lifestyle and can instead put down roots and raise a family. The conflict in the film is their ability to adopt a child, not the viability of the show itself. In the end, it is their stability as a married couple working in television that allows them to adopt multiple children at once.

White Christmas is another case in point. While the film celebrates live entertainment and demonstrates, like *Rebecca of Sunnybrook Farm*, that country values and city values can be successfully integrated, it also acknowledges the power of television to influence audiences. In a critical scene, Bob Wallace (Bing Crosby) arranges to appear on the *Ed Harrison Show* in order to recruit an audience to celebrate their friend Major General Thomas Waverly (Dean Jagger). General Waverly is retired and feels forgotten by the men he commanded during World War II. With a television appearance in which Bob sings an homage to retired generals everywhere, "What Do

You Do with a General?," he hopes to reach as many of his friend's division as possible. As he sings, the film cuts to his estranged girlfriend Betty (Rosemary Clooney) watching the broadcast. She is emotionally moved by his heartfelt plea. In this moment, the musical registers its incorporation of television itself. The shot is a close-up of the television set, a wooden console table with the black-and-white screen at the center. Bob stands in the middle singing directly to the audience on the other side of the monitor. Musical film and televisual entertainment become one, and Bing Crosby, an actor closely associated with the genre's evolution, functions as its mediator.

Those musicals that are set far away from the stage have also reckoned with the coming of new technologies and modes of communication. In particular, the folk musical, with its nostalgic orientation backward in time and its celebration of family, community, and cultural ritual, has been most interested in exploring the intrusion of modernity into otherwise-pastoral spaces. Folk musicals like *Meet Me in St. Louis* (Vincente Minnelli, 1944), *Summer Holiday* (Rouben Mamoulian, 1948), and *The Music Man* (Morton DaCosta, 1962) idealize the American small town at the turn of the century. Families and communities take on primary importance as stable relationships that provide a bulwark to imminent changes around them. In *Meet Me in St. Louis*, it is the father's quest for a better job that will uproot the Smith family from their beloved home. In *Summer Holiday*, it is the young son's restlessness and desire for adventure that threaten the family's happiness. And in *The Music Man*, it is the arrival of a stranger from out of town that upsets the normal patterns of everyday life (see Garcia 2014).

A central project of such films is to show how family and community reckon with and integrate these unfamiliar objects into their lives as a means of strengthening their connections to one another. The telephone disrupts the family dinner in *Meet Me in St. Louis* and produces a less-than-satisfactory experience for the oldest daughter and her beau, who are separated from each other. But other new forms, like the trolley, bring the young people of the town together for a rollicking good time as they sing "The Trolley Song" on their way to the fairground. In *Summer Holiday*, the Stanley Steamer, a steam-engine-powered car, allows space for the entire family to ride in it as they sing, "Honk, honk, honk! / The tandem bike has had its day / If you're ridin' one you'll find that they / Poke along in an obsolete way." Here they celebrate what new technology has given them, just as in *The Music Man* when the entire town excitedly sings while waiting for the Wells Fargo wagon. In the number "The Wells Fargo Wagon," the town expresses its joy at receiving items like maple sugar, a bathtub, curtains, and a double boiler, embracing this new home-delivery service that connects them to the broader landscape of American consumerism. Most importantly, the Wells Fargo wagon brings the band instruments to the young boys of the town, which diverts their attention away from less edifying pursuits like playing pool and strengthens the community as a whole. The folk musical renders these new forms of communication not only as unthreatening but also as generative to group cohesion and identity.

LISTENING

In John Carney's musical films, the mediation of music is communication itself. Throughout *Sing Street*, a film about teenagers coming of age in Ireland in the 1980s, the main character, Conor (Ferdia Walsh-Peelo), has difficulty connecting to Raphina (Lucy Boynton), an elusive young woman who lives at a home for girls across from his school. She seems old for her age. She is independent and confident in her posturing as an up-and-coming model. Her inscrutability inspires Conor to create a band. Along with his bandmate Eamon (Mark McKenna), Conor writes songs about her, first "The Riddle of the Model" and then "Up." He delivers both recordings to her on a cassette tape, which becomes his primary means of emotional expression.

The act of listening is a central form of encounter and communication in *Sing Street*. For the second song, "Up," Carney establishes how Conor and Raphina are coming closer together via the song on the cassette tape. The sequence begins with the band playing the song in Eamon's living room. At the chorus, "It's such a beautiful feelin' / Goin' up / She lights me up," the film cuts to Conor riding his bike down Raphina's dark street. He drops off the cassette, wrapped in brown paper, through the mail slot in her front door while the music continues to play on the soundtrack. The film cuts again to Raphina in her room, turning over the wrapped tape. We watch in close-up as she inserts it into her cassette player and presses play. She smiles while she listens, tying her hair back, and sitting at her vanity table while she wipes off her makeup. The film cuts back to the band performing the song in daylight and then again to Raphina in the evening. This time, as she listens, she begins to cry, moved by what she hears. The final shot of the sequence belongs to the next scene. As the song dies out, we see Conor walking to school. He has dyed his hair and put on eye makeup. The song serenades Raphina as she takes off her makeup and becomes vulnerable enough to show emotion, while it inspires Conor to confidently express himself in new ways. Through the material object of the cassette, the film links Conor and Raphina across time

THE MUSICAL AS MEDIATION · 97

and space, from the boy's living room by day to her bedroom by night.

These sound bridges play an important role in all of Carney's work. Rick Altman (1987) has pointed out how Hollywood musicals use audio and visual dissolves in order to bridge the divide between the narrative and musical sequences. For example, music might begin diegetically in a musical, get elevated to a supradiegetic level in which the music continues but with additional instrumentation not visible as a source within the film, and then return ultimately to the diegetic realm. Matthew J. Fee shows in his analysis of *Once* how Carney's use of sound bridges accomplishes something different: instead of leading us back to the space of performance, Carney leads us outward "to return us to a story very clearly located in contemporary Dublin" (2010, 182). Carney's bridges do move us through space, foregrounding the urban locales in which his characters move. But such sound bridges function more broadly in the film. They are tools for achieving an interconnectivity made possible by a continuous musical track that extends over the characters' world, defying spatiotemporal boundaries. In uniting instances of playing and listening to music in the same sequence, Carney renders them as continuous actions that aurally and visually unite his characters. In *Sing Street,* the cassette functions as a metonymic symbol of Conor's feelings and the literal means by which young people commune with one another. When the cassette cannot be shared, as near the end, it is a signal that Raphina has abruptly left Ireland and that their connection has broken.

A smartphone, headphones, earbuds, and a splitter are the mediating objects for a listening scene in *Begin Again*. Dan and Gretta sit in his car. Hanging from his rearview mirror is a splitter, which he explains is "for two headphones going into one input" and was significant during his first date with his wife. "We walked all over the city listening to her CD player," he recalls. "I don't think we said more than two words to each other the whole night." That experience, he says, led to their marriage two months later. Now estranged from his wife and living separately from her, he finds a sympathetic listener in Gretta. In order to get to know her better, he asks, "What kind of music do you have on your phone?"—indicating that the means by which we listen to music has changed over time. She resists the intrusive move ("I'm not giving you access to my music library"). Persistent, Dan suggests, "You can tell a lot about a person by what is on their playlist." Gretta acquiesces, and the two walk through the city listening to each other's songs by way of the splitter and their cell phones.

Again, Carney uses music to bridge time and space. They begin with one of her songs, Frank Sinatra's "Luck Be a Lady," as they walk through Times Square. The camera follows them from a low angle, capturing Gretta's glances upward to the lights on the billboards and marquees. A jump cut finds them coming out of a subway station and listening to one of Dan's choices, Stevie Wonder's "For Once in My Life," a song that inspires them to dance. Another cut reveals them in a dance club, where loud house music is playing and people crowd the dance floor. Once the film cuts to Gretta's face, however, Stevie Wonder's song overcomes the soundtrack, and the two of them dance to their own music while still being part of a crowd. The song continues, and the film cuts forward and backward in time and across space, capturing them standing silently on the subway, walking along a sidewalk, back on the subway, sitting on a stoop, and sitting closely together on the subway car's long bench while rubbing their shoulders together in tandem with the song's syncopation. For the final moment, they go to Central Park and listen to a song from her favorite film, *Casablanca* (Michael Curtiz, 1942), Dooley Wilson's performance of "As Time Goes By." The song reverberates over their walk through the park and to an intersection where they sit to watch the passersby. He moves his headphones to expose one ear, and she takes out one of her earbuds so they can talk and listen at the same time. Watching the pedestrian traffic, Dan explains, "All these banalities, they suddenly turn into these beautiful, effervescent pearls . . . from music." Wilson's song provides a romantic soundtrack to cops leading away a drunk person, a woman walking in stilettos, a man on a bicycle, a group of Hare Krishnas standing on a corner, and a lone man walking down the street. And finally, it serenades the two characters as they walk away from the camera holding hands.

The splitter makes their enjoyable evening possible, as does their ability to carry hundreds of MP3 files on their smartphones wherever they go. But instead of bemoaning the lack of authenticity in digital music or the ways that smartphone devices can make us asocial beings, Carney embraces the potential of these new technologies. In his work, digital music, smartphones, and a splitter allow for music to be the thing that is always there across time and space. Its easy accessibility means that the world can become a musical. Declaring the diegetic source of the musical does nothing to take away from the feelings of transcendence in this sequence precisely because we see the music's effect on the characters. We encounter the world through their ears. Finally, while there is little dialogue in this scene, as was the case with Dan's first date with his wife, the characters share themselves with each other through their music, establishing a deep connection that then becomes a romantic encounter.

CREATING

In Carney's films, creating music often leads to listening, and listening often leads to musical creation. Both are central to establishing human connection. In a scene in *Once*, the Guy (Glen Hansard) and the Girl (Markéta Irglová) have only recently met. He is a busker, a street musician, singing and strumming his guitar on the corner for change, and she is a Czech immigrant who works multiple jobs but occasionally finds time to play the piano. The two enter a music store, a place where she has permission to practice her music. She asks him to play her one of his songs as she sits at the piano. He obliges, instructing her on the chords and the melody ("It goes, 'da da da da'"). She plays the melody on the piano, and he follows with the bridge, to which she adds some notes. Asking if she wants to give it a spin, the Guy invites her to create the song with him. They begin to sing and play together. The Girl initially only contributes the melody, but gradually her chords become more complex and she switches to singing harmony to his vocals. By the time they get to the chorus, which he announces ("Take this sinking boat / and point it home / we've still got time"), they are fully collaborating on the song, melding their voices and instruments together. They smile at each other along the way, having achieved this moment of musical communion. Confirming the song's persuasive powers, the camera provides a single cutaway shot of the shop owner glancing toward them with a slight grin. Constantly keeping in view the shop's wall of musical instruments, both electric and acoustic guitars, the scene establishes the space as one that is pregnant with the possibilities for creation.

Carney's handheld camera is dynamic, slightly bobbing as it moves around the two characters. It holds them in a medium shot, alternating vantage points on either side of the piano. As the song returns to the verse ("Falling slowly"), the camera moves forward for a close-up of the Guy and then out again. It tracks across the back of the piano to frame the both of them once more before moving into the Girl's close-up and out again. In this way, the film visually establishes the budding relationship of the two characters, echoing the work being done by their collaboration on the song itself. The scene's perpetual motion also allows for multiple subject positions for the audience, never allowing us to remain stationary. As it realigns and repositions, following the ebbs and flows of the song itself, the sequence gives the audience a sense of taking part in this musical creation. But while the store provides the site of origination for the song, it is not confined to that place. The characters leave, and a sound bridge continues the song's instrumental riff as they walk through city streets and ride a bus. Music, like Carney's camera, is dynamic and mobile and infuses the characters' entire world.

The Guy and the Girl continue their process of collaboration even when they are apart from each other. As we see in a subsequent scene, the Guy hands the Girl a CD on which he has recorded a new melody and lends her his Discman and headphones so that she can listen to it and possibly write some lyrics. As with the cassette tape in *Sing Street*, the Discman becomes the mediating device to connect the characters musically and emotionally. But because of its materiality, it has the potential to fail, thereby disrupting the musical moment. The Girl listens to the CD in her bedroom while her infant daughter sleeps in a nearby crib. She quietly mouths some lyrics, but inconveniently, the batteries die. "Fuck you, batteries," she exclaims as she searches through the house in vain for replacements. She takes some change out of her daughter's piggy bank, with a glance toward the crib and a promise to pay her back, and ventures out into the street in pajamas and robe to the corner store. The Girl immediately inserts the new batteries into the Discman and begins to listen to the song as she heads home.

Shot on digital video, the film has a documentary feel throughout, but it is especially acute in this sequence. The camera captures a group of young girls who are roller-skating outside the convenience store. They gawk at the camera and at the Girl as she sings to herself while listening to the Discman. Some of them follow her down the street. Their presence calls attention to the song happening in real time and in real space as the camera tracks backward, keeping her in the frame all the while. As she goes, we see her neighborhood, the real streets in Dublin, with its cars and traffic lights and pedestrians who frame her backdrop. But like the splitter scene in *Begin Again*, this moment renders reality as a musical. We go from hearing only her voice to hearing what she is hearing as well. It is an introspective moment for the character. The Girl stays focused on the lyrics she has written on a piece of paper and occasionally glances around her. But even though she is the only character in the scene, Carney makes it clear that she is not alone. The music to which she sings is the Guy's, and her addition of lyrics makes this a moment in which we see musical collaboration happening before us. The addition of the Guy's voice in harmony with her own indicates that they are together if nonetheless physically apart. Again, Carney's films use music to transcend time and space. The number ends with a sound bridge that extends to future moments when the characters are apart—she cleans a house, he makes a meal for his father—but the continuous soundtrack makes it clear that they are still connected to each other.

In each of Carney's films, individuals become a band. The creation that occurs pertains not only to music but also to a collective. In *Once*, the Guy and the Girl recruit other street musicians to collaborate on an album. In *Begin Again*, the band is a combination of amateurs, students, and professionals, including music students, street musicians, children, Dan's daughter, and a bass player and drummer from Cee Lo Green's band (Cee Lo plays himself as Dan's friend and advocate). And in *Sing Street*, the band is a group of high school students from Synge Street Academy, a Catholic school that Conor must attend as a result of his family's reduced finances. The kids are a group of outcasts. Conor is the new kid in school. He meets Eamon, who is reclusive but a musical wunderkind. Along with his friend Darren (Ben Carolan), a diminutive teenager who assumes the role of manager, they make the assumption that the one black kid in school, Ngig (Percy Chamburuka), must know how to play an instrument ("He'll be able to play somethin'. He's black!"). In this way, the scene references an earlier Irish musical, *The Commitments* (Alan Parker, 1991), in which a newly formed band watches footage of James Brown in order to understand how to have "soul." But the automatic association between blackness and musicality does not go without comment in *Sing Street*. When Darren casually uses racial epithets, Conor corrects him, a sign of the differences in their social backgrounds. Moreover, the boys' erroneous assumption that Ngig cannot speak English gets quickly dispelled. Ngig demonstrates that he can indeed play the electric keyboard and earns himself a place in the band as the only black and immigrant member. Completing the group's formation, two other socially marginalized kids, taunted as "faggots" by an older student, also join the group.

In the band's first instance of playing together, Carney's camera pans around them, communicating each student's musical skills along the way. In these instances when bands are formed and come together as one, music and musical instruments are the tools for creating community where there was none. The bands are transformative for the characters in all of Carney's films. They instill pride and confidence in individuals who are otherwise socially adrift, they produce art, and they create social worlds with song and musical instruments as their primary mode of communication.

PLAYING

Carney's musicals eschew the performance of music for the playing of music. Given that their stories focus on characters who are musicians and singers, it would follow that moments of performance, in which those characters successfully entertain an audience, would be an important part of the narrative structure. A central device of Hollywood's backstage-musical tradition, a performance before an audience justifies the entertainment paid for and being given. Such scenes are few and far between in Carney's work. Music should not be confined to a commercial stage, his films suggest. His characters go to great lengths to find music in the ordinary and the everyday. They make do with what is available to them. The Girl in *Once* borrows a piano in the music store. The Guy plays his well-worn guitar on Dublin's street corners. Conor in *Sing Street* uses the vacuum hose from his friend's Hoover to create a reverb effect. And Gretta in *Begin Again* uses city streets as ambient sound on her album. After turning down a recording deal, she places the album online to sell for only one dollar. In other words, music can be listened to and created outside the mainstream. Carney's musicals reject the notion that only professionals can make music and that music itself is a commercial product. Removing the audience, the focus moves toward the experience of playing music rather than the performance of it. Anyone, Carney seems to suggest, can do it themselves.

These films go further to revise the musical's conventional use of a diegetic audience. Indeed, the audience per se only appears in two of Carney's musicals and both in atypical ways. In *Begin Again*, as mentioned earlier in this chapter, the commercial world of performance and audience falls under scrutiny. Gretta and Dave (Adam Levine) have come to New York from London because he has a record deal after having a featured song in a popular film. Their paths diverge quickly, however, when Dave succumbs to the allure of American consumerism and stardom. He cheats on Gretta, which she immediately intuits when he plays her a new song he has written. Music continues to be the language with which she communicates with him after they have broken up. She uses her smartphone to call him and leave a voicemail that consists not of spoken words but of a song she has written about their breakup. At the end of the film, Dave performs a live concert at the Gramercy Theatre. He has invited Gretta to join him onstage for the song that she has written. As she watches him from the wings, deciding whether to join him, the film offers a point-of-view shot of the adoring fans, mostly women, who gaze up at Dave and reach out to him worshipfully. Her vantage point makes it clear that his musical world is not hers. As she states early in the film, "music is about the ears, not eyes." She exits the theater, rejecting the possibility of a personal and musical connection with her ex-boyfriend. In the end, her practice of playing music, organically and without profit, and Dave's highly orchestrated performance are at odds. Unlike other musical films in which the guy and girl come together in the end in a stage-bound musical performance, *Begin Again* finds Gretta alone but with her commitment to the personal and communal approach to music intact.

Carney qualifies his view of musical performance with *Sing Street*, demonstrating how video can be valuable to the dissemination of music. Early in the film, Conor's mother (Maria Doyle Kennedy) calls him and his brother, Brendan (Jack Reynor), to the living room to watch *Top of the Pops*. As a family, they interact with the Duran Duran music video "Rio," which takes place on a tropical beach and on a sailboat. The father voices his critique of this new medium: "If this is the future, we're all screwed, aren't we? I mean, look at this guy—he's not even singing live." Brendan defends the video: "It's art! This lasts forever. It's the perfect mixture of music and visuals." There is a mediated circularity that this conflict references; just like *Footlight Parade* and *Babes in Arms* self-consciously allude to the musical film's replacement of live performance, the allure of the music video threatens the live concert. Carney cuts between the family and the television screen, eventually filling the frame with Duran Duran's video while Brendan concludes, "I mean, what tyranny would stand up to that?" The video's fracturing of linearity and perspective, its use of distorted imagery and side-by-side frames of action, suggest the rejection of sanctioned forms of authority. Even though the father does not understand (he says, "they're no Beatles!"), Carney conveys how music videos merely continue the historical function of rock music, to foment rebellion among youth. The television set and the music video constitute the two forms of mediation in this sequence, between old and new forms of culture and between generations. And we see how the video inspires Conor to create with his band. Their first video, "The Riddle of the Model," replicates Duran Duran's mystification of a female figure in "Rio." But in this process, we also come to understand how making music videos, like making music, is a democratic process of making meaningful forms of art for the individual and for the group.

The theme of rebellion continues to the end of the film. Conor and his band perform at a school dance. At rehearsal, he anxiously anticipates Raphina's arrival. When she does not appear, the band goes forward anyway, singing "Drive It like You Stole It," and imagines a dance hall from the 1950s in which men and women in midcentury dress perform a choreographed dance to the song. The number is closest to those that appear in Hollywood musicals, where unity is created between the performers and the audience through shared song and dance. The musical number fixes any number of social problems raised in the film. Raphina appears on the dance floor and gazes adoringly at Conor while he sings. His parents, who have in fact separated due to infidelity, appear happily dancing together and cheering him on. But when the song ends abruptly, the dance floor is mostly empty, the bright colors of their 1950s clothing are gone, and Conor's personal problems continue. While the sequence is light and buoyant, replicating the feelings of elation elicited by any number of musical films prior, it rebels against the form, acknowledging that such a world is only make-believe and, perhaps, only made possible by the fictional world of musical film.

Making due with reality, the band performs an actual act of rebellion with their last number. Conor, who had been physically and nearly sexually abused by a Catholic priest at his school, has written the song "Brown Shoes," a reference to his failure to wear the sanctioned black shoes to school, which then evolves into an act of insurgence. Dedicating the song "to every Christian brother and every bully you ever knew," the band performs the number while wearing masks of the priest's face. They have made dozens of them and throw them at the audience of students, who put them on while dancing to the song. The sequence is the band's last not only because the priest has made it clear that they will never perform there again but also because Conor and Raphina plan to leave home in order to pursue their dreams in London. Like the characters in the Duran Duran video, they set sail to make art.

Carney uses performance sequences to demystify them. In the first school-dance number, the director shows how musical numbers have the tendency to assuage social realities, but the idyllic world created by the musical cannot be sustained. Like the music video itself, musical performance has the power to disrupt and challenge forms of authority. And music, rock 'n' roll in this case, is a form of mediation central to human expression and relationships.

The musical has long grappled with its original sin of replacing silent cinema, featuring songs for marketability, and the removal of an audience-performer connection. Its reflection on its own material constitution, as sound cinema that employs audiovisual techniques in the creation of entertainment, has been a perpetual theme in musical films themselves. As the genre evolved and new forms of media emerged that had the potential to challenge the movie musical, filmmakers showed how these too could be incorporated into the genre's project of integration.

In *Once, Begin Again,* and *Sing Street,* John Carney features music as a mediating device that overcomes feelings of alienation in favor of community. Extending the genre's focus to forms of media, he employs analog and digital objects as critical devices for human connection in the twenty-first century. Through listening, creating, and playing, his characters overcome boundaries of time and space in order to engage in an alternate, and fundamentally musical, form of communication.

Moreover, Carney's musicals place music in the hands of the ordinary person. Encounters with music happen in everyday contexts like the street and the home. In this way, his films echo larger cultural transformations that have shaped the late twentieth and early twenty-first centuries. The creation of the home-video market domesticated musical-film spectatorship and the tradition of community singing in the theater. With the release of VHS tapes in the 1980s and DVDs in the 1990s, the earliest of which included sing-along tracks to Disney films and the musicals from Hollywood's golden age, families could encounter and participate in the musical number themselves. More recently, the public sing-along phenomenon, in which song lyrics display for twenty-first-century screenings of *The Sound of Music* (1965), *Frozen* (2013), and *The Greatest Showman* (2017), demonstrates the extent to which technology can function in service to community creation. In an ever evolving form, the musical brings people together onscreen and off, in public venues and in private living rooms. Going forward, we may not know how new technologies will shape our encounters with the world and with each other, but we can be certain that the musical will be there to assist with their mediation.

ACKNOWLEDGMENTS

As this book quickly demonstrates, *The Movie Musical* is inspired by and indebted to generations of scholars of musical film. Their adamant attention to the genre and careful consideration of its form and history have enabled my own persistent focus on the many ways the musical is more than just entertainment. I am appreciative of these scholars' vision and of the ways they continue to chart a path forward for others to follow.

I am profoundly grateful to Rutgers University Press and especially to Leslie Mitchener, who first extended the invitation to write this volume. And thank you to Nicole Solano for patiently steering me through the publication process and to the Quick Takes series editors, Gwendolyn Audrey Foster and Wheeler Winston Dixon, for their enthusiasm and guidance. I am also deeply appreciative of the external reviewer's time and effort it took to read the book in draft form. The book is better for that process.

Prior to the book's publication, multiple versions of these chapters appeared in other venues and forms. Thank you to Cynthia Lucia and the students and faculty at Rider University who hosted me for their annual Film Symposium and helped me to work out my idea of the musical as an archive. And I benefited enormously from the feedback at the Columbia Seminar on Cinema and Interdisciplinary Interpretation, organized by Bill Luhrs and Cynthia Lucia, and especially from the critique offered by Paula J. Massood.

I am grateful to Justin Hurwitz and Damien Chazelle for helping to clarify and explain their choices behind certain scenes in *La La Land*.

And finally and always, my love and appreciation goes to my two screening partners, Edith Aliza and Matthew.

FURTHER READING

Altman, Rick. *The American Film Musical*. Bloomington: Indiana University Press, 1987.

Avila, Jacqueline. *Cinesonidos: Film Music and National Identity during Mexico's Época de Oro*. New York: Oxford University Press, 2019.

Backstein, Karen. "'Stayin' Alive': The Post-Studio Hollywood Musical." In *American Film History: Selected Readings, 1960 to the Present*, edited by Cynthia Lucia, Roy Grundmann, and Art Simon, 286–303. Chichester, UK: Wiley-Blackwell, 2015.

Barrios, Richard. *A Song in the Dark: The Birth of the Musical Film*. Oxford: Oxford University Press, 1995.

Becker, Svea, and Bruce Williams. "What Ever Happened to *West Side Story*? Gene Kelly, Jazz Dance, and Not So Real Men in Jacques Demy's *The Young Girls of Rochefort*." *New Review of Film and Television Studies* 6.3 (2008): 303–21.

Brannigan, Erin. *Dancefilm: Choreography and the Moving Image*. New York: Oxford University Press, 2011.

Cohan, Steven. "'Feminizing' the Song-and-Dance Man: Fred Astaire and the Spectacle of Masculinity in the Hollywood Musical." In *Hollywood Musicals: The Film Reader*, edited by Steven Cohan, 87–102. New York: Routledge, 2002.

Cohan, Steven. *Hollywood by Hollywood: The Backstudio Picture and the Mystique of Making Movies*. New York: Oxford University Press, 2019.

———. *Hollywood Musicals*. New York: Routledge, 2019.

———. *Incongruous Entertainment: Camp, Cultural Value, and the MGM Musical*. Durham, NC: Duke University Press, 2005.

———, ed. *The Sound of Musicals*. London: British Film Institute, 2010.

Creekmur, Corey K., and Linda Y. Mokdad. *The International Film Musical*. Edinburgh: Edinburgh University Press, 2013.

Dyer, Richard. "Entertainment and Utopia." In *Hollywood Musicals: The Film Reader*, edited by Steven Cohan, 19–30. New York: Routledge, 2002.

———. *In the Space of a Song: The Uses of Song in Film*. New York: Routledge, 2011.

Farmer, Brett. "The Singing Sixties: Rethinking the Julie Andrews Roadshow Musical." In *The Sound of Musicals*, edited by Steven Cohan, 114–27. London: British Film Institute, 2010.

Fee, Matthew J. "'A Musical Dressed Up in a Different Way': Urban Ireland and the Possible Spaces of John Carney's *Once*." In *The Sound of Musicals*, edited by Steven Cohan, 176–87. London: British Film Institute, 2010.

Feuer, Jane. *The Hollywood Musical*. Bloomington: Indiana University Press, 1993.

———. "The International Art Musical: Defining and Periodising Post-1980s Musicals." In *The Sound of Musicals*, edited by Steven Cohan, 54–63. London: British Film Institute, 2010.

———. "Is *Dirty Dancing* a Musical, and Why Should It Matter?" In *The Time of Our Lives: "Dirty Dancing" and Popular Culture*, edited by Yannis Tzioumakis and Sian Lincoln, 59–72. Detroit: Wayne State University Press, 2013.

———. "The Self-Reflective Musical and the Myth of Entertainment." In *Hollywood Musicals: The Film Reader*, edited by Steven Cohan, 31–40. New York: Routledge, 2002.

Fleeger, Jennifer. *Mismatched Women: The Siren's Song through the Machine*. New York: Oxford University Press, 2014.

Flinn, Caryl. "The Music of Screen Musicals." In *The Cambridge Companion to Film Music*, edited by Mervyn Cooke and Fiona Ford, 231–46. Cambridge: Cambridge University Press, 2016.

———. *The Sound of Music*. London: Palgrave, 2015.

Friedman, Ryan Jay. *Hollywood's African American Films: The Transition to Sound*. New Brunswick, NJ: Rutgers University Press, 2011.

Gabbard, Krin. *Jammin' at the Margins: Jazz and the American Cinema*. Chicago: University of Chicago Press, 1996.

———. "*La La Land* Is a Hit, but Is It Good for Jazz?" *Daedalus: Journal of the American Academy of Arts and Sciences* 148.2 (Spring 2019): 92–103.

Gallefant, Edward. *Astaire Rogers*. New York: Columbia University Press, 2002.

Garcia, Desirée J. *The Migration of Musical Film: From Ethnic Margins to American Mainstream.* New Brunswick, NJ: Rutgers University Press, 2014.

Gopal, Sangita, and Sujata Moorti. "Bollywood in Drag: *Moulin Rouge!* and the Aesthetics of Global Cinema." *Camera Obscura* 25.3(75) (2011): 29–67.

———. *Global Bollywood: Travels of Hindi Song and Dance.* Minneapolis: University of Minnesota Press, 2008.

Grant, Barry K. "The Classic Hollywood Musical and the 'Problem' of Rock 'n' Roll." *Journal of Popular Film and Television* 13.4 (Winter 1986): 196–205.

———. *The Hollywood Film Musical.* Chichester, UK: Wiley-Blackwell, 2012.

Griffin, Sean. *Free and Easy? A Defining History of the American Film Musical Genre.* Chichester, UK: Wiley-Blackwell, 2018.

———. "The Gang's All Here: Generic versus Racial Integration in the 1940s Musical." *Cinema Journal* 42.1 (Fall 2002): 21–45.

Herzog, Amy. *Dreams of Difference, Songs of the Same: The Musical Moment in Film.* Minneapolis: University of Minnesota Press, 2010.

Kalinak, Kathryn. "From *The Jazz Singer* to *La La Land* and Some Others in Between." In *Identity Mediations in Latin American Cinema and Beyond,* edited by Cecilia Nuria Gil Mariño and Laura Miranda, 128–51. Newcastle-upon-Tyne, UK: Cambridge Scholars, 2019.

Kennedy, Matthew. *Roadshow! The Fall of Film Musicals in the 1960s.* Oxford: Oxford University Press, 2014.

Kessler, Kelly. *Broadway in the Box: Television's Lasting Love Affair with the Musical*. New York: Oxford University Press, 2020.

———. *Destabilizing the Hollywood Musical: Music, Masculinity and Mayhem*. Basingstoke, UK: Macmillan, 2010.

Knight, Arthur. *Disintegrating the Musical: Black Performance and American Musical Film*. Durham, NC: Duke University Press, 2002.

Ma, Jean. *Sounding the Modern Woman: The Songstress in Chinese Cinema*. Durham, NC: Duke University Press, 2015.

Marshall, Bill, and Robynn Stillwell, eds. *Musicals: Hollywood and Beyond*. Exeter, UK: Intellect, 2000.

Martin, Adrian. "Musical Mutations: Before, Beyond and Against Hollywood." In *Movie Mutations: The Changing Face of World Cinephilia*, edited by Jonathan Rosenbaum and Adrian Martin, 94–108. London: British Film Institute, 2003.

McElhaney, Joe. 2018. "Alain Resnais, Tsai Ming-liang, and the Apartment Plot Musical." In *The Apartment Complex: Urban Living and Global Screen Cultures*, edited by Pamela Robertson Wojcik, 65–83. Durham, NC: Duke University Press.

McLean, Adrienne L. *Being Rita Hayworth: Labor, Identity, and Hollywood Stardom*. New Brunswick, NJ: Rutgers University Press, 2004.

———. *Dying Swans and Madmen: Ballet, the Body, and Narrative Cinema*. New Brunswick, NJ: Rutgers University Press, 2008.

Mordden, Ethan. *The Hollywood Musical*. New York: St. Martin's, 1981.

Mundy, John. *The British Musical Film*. Manchester, UK: Manchester University Press, 2007.

Norðfjörð, Björn. "The Post-modern Transnational Film Musical." In *The International Film Musical*, edited by Corey K. Creekmur and Linda Y. Mokdad, 241–56. Edinburgh: Edinburgh University Press, 2013.

O'Brien, Charles. *Movies, Songs, and Electric Sound*. Bloomington: Indiana University Press, 2019.

Oyallon-Koloski, Jenny. "Genre Experimentation and Contemporary Dance in *Jeanne et le garçon formidable*." *Studies in French Cinema* 14.2 (2014): 91–107.

Petty, Miriam J. *Stealing the Show: African American Performers and Audiences in 1930s Hollywood*. Berkeley: University of California Press, 2016.

Rubin, Martin. *Showstoppers: Busby Berkeley and the Tradition of Spectacle*. New York: Columbia University Press, 1993.

Shearer, Martha. *New York City and the Hollywood Musical: Dancing in the Streets*. London: Palgrave Macmillan, 2016.

Smith, Susan. *The Musical: Race, Gender and Performance*. London: Wallflower, 2005.

Spring, Katherine. *Saying It with Songs: Popular Music and the Coming of Sound to Hollywood Cinema*. New York: Oxford University Press, 2014.

Whitesell, Lloyd. *Wonderful Design: Glamour in the Hollywood Musical*. New York: Oxford University Press, 2018.

Woods Peiró, Eva. *White Gypsies: Race and Stardom in Spanish Musicals*. Minneapolis: University of Minnesota Press, 2012.

REFERENCES

Altman, Rick. 1987. *The American Film Musical*. Blooming-
    ton: Indiana University Press.

Backstein, Karen. 2015. "'Stayin' Alive': The Post-Studio
    Hollywood Musical." In *American Film History: Selected
    Readings, 1960 to the Present*, edited by Cynthia Lucia,
    Roy Grundmann, and Art Simon, 286–303. Chichester,
    UK: Wiley-Blackwell.

Cameron, Allan. 2012. "Zombie Media: Transmission,
    Reproduction, and the Digital Dead." *Cinema Journal*
    52.1 (Fall): 68–89.

Cohan, Steven. 2002. "'Feminizing' the Song-and-Dance
    Man: Fred Astaire and the Spectacle of Masculinity in
    the Hollywood Musical." In *Hollywood Musicals: The
    Film Reader*, edited by Steven Cohan, 87–102. New York:
    Routledge.

———, ed. 2010. *The Sound of Musicals*. London: British
    Film Institute.

———. 2019a. *Hollywood by Hollywood: The Backstudio
    Picture and the Mystique of Making Movies*. New York:
    Oxford University Press.

———. 2019b. *Hollywood Musicals*. New York: Routledge.

Creekmur, Corey K., and Linda Y. Mokdad. 2013. *The Inter-
    national Film Musical*. Edinburgh: Edinburgh University
    Press.

Dyer, Richard. 2002. "Entertainment and Utopia." In *Hollywood Musicals: The Film Reader*, edited by Steven Cohan, 19–30. New York: Routledge.

Farmer, Brett. 2010. "The Singing Sixties: Rethinking the Julie Andrews Roadshow Musical." In *The Sound of Musicals*, edited by Steven Cohan, 114–27. London: British Film Institute.

Fee, Matthew J. 2010. "'A Musical Dressed Up in a Different Way': Urban Ireland and the Possible Spaces of John Carney's *Once*." In *The Sound of Musicals*, edited by Steven Cohan, 176–87. London: British Film Institute.

Feuer, Jane. 1982. *The Hollywood Musical*. Bloomington: Indiana University Press.

———. 2002. "The Self-Reflective Musical and the Myth of Entertainment." In *Hollywood Musicals: The Film Reader*, edited by Steven Cohan, 31–40. New York: Routledge.

———. 2010. "The International Art Musical: Defining and Periodising Post-1980s Musicals." In *The Sound of Musicals*, edited by Steven Cohan, 54–63. London: British Film Institute.

Flinn, Caryl. 2016. "The Music of Screen Musicals." In *The Cambridge Companion to Film Music*, edited by Mervyn Cooke and Fiona Ford, 231–46. Cambridge: Cambridge University Press.

Gabbard, Krin. 1996. *Jammin' at the Margins: Jazz and the American Cinema*. Chicago: University of Chicago Press.

———. 2019. "*La La Land* Is a Hit, but Is It Good for Jazz?" *Daedalus: Journal of the American Academy of Arts and Sciences* 148.2 (Spring): 92–103.

Gallefant, Edward. 2002. *Astaire Rogers.* New York: Columbia University Press.

Garcia, Desirée J. 2014. *The Migration of Musical Film: From Ethnic Margins to American Mainstream.* New Brunswick, NJ: Rutgers University Press.

Gopal, Sangita, and Sujata Moorit. 2011. "Bollywood in Drag: *Moulin Rouge!* and the Aesthetics of Global Cinema." *Camera Obscura* 25.3(75): 29–67.

Grant, Barry K. 1986. "The Classic Hollywood Musical and the 'Problem' of Rock 'n' Roll." *Journal of Popular Film and Television* 13.4 (Winter): 196–205.

———. 2012. *The Hollywood Film Musical.* Chichester, UK: Wiley-Blackwell.

Griffin, Sean. 2002. "The Gang's All Here: Generic versus Racial Integration in the 1940s Musical." *Cinema Journal* 42.1 (Fall): 21–45.

———. 2018. *Free and Easy? A Defining History of the American Film Musical Genre.* Chichester, UK: Wiley-Blackwell.

Jameson, Fredric. 1998. *The Cultural Turn: Selected Writings on the Postmodern, 1983–1998.* London: Verso.

Joyrich, Lynn. 1988. "All That Television Allows: TV Melodrama, Postmodernism and Consumer Culture." *Camera Obscura* 6.1 (16): 128–53.

Kael, Pauline. 1968. *Kiss Kiss Bang Bang.* Boston: Little, Brown.

Kalinak, Kathryn. 2019. "From *The Jazz Singer* to *La La Land* and Some Others in Between." In *Identity Mediations in Latin American Cinema and Beyond,* edited by Cecilia Nuria Gil Mariño and Laura Miranda, 128–51. Newcastle-upon-Tyne, UK: Cambridge Scholars.

Kennedy, Matthew. 2014. *Roadshow! The Fall of Film Musicals in the 1960s.* Oxford: Oxford University Press.

Kessler, Kelly. 2010. *Destabilizing the Hollywood Musical: Music, Masculinity and Mayhem.* Basingstoke, UK: Macmillan.

———. 2020. *Broadway in the Box: Television's Lasting Love Affair with the Musical.* Oxford: Oxford University Press.

Levine, Lawrence. 1992. "The Folklore of Industrial Society: Popular Culture and Its Audiences." *American Historical Review* 97.5 (December): 1369–99.

Limon, John. 2016. "Escapism; or, The Soul of Globalization." *Genre* 49.1 (April): 51–77.

Ma, Jean. 2015. *Sounding the Modern Woman: The Songstress in Chinese Cinema.* Durham, NC: Duke University Press.

Martin, Adrian. 2003. "Musical Mutations: Before, Beyond and Against Hollywood." In *Movie Mutations: The Changing Face of World Cinephilia*, edited by Jonathan Rosenbaum and Adrian Martin, 94–108. London: British Film Institute.

Metz, Christian. 1974. *Language and Cinema.* The Hague: Mouton.

Mulvey, Laura. 1975. "Visual Pleasure and Narrative Cinema." *Screen* 16.3 (Autumn): 6–18.

Neale, Steve. 2006. "'The Last Good Time We Ever Had?': Revising the Hollywood Renaissance." In *Contemporary American Cinema*, edited by Linda Ruth Williams and Michael Hammond, 90–92. Maidenhead, UK: Open University Press.

Norðfjörð, Björn. 2013. "The Post-modern Transnational Film Musical." In *The International Film Musical*, edited by Corey K. Creekmur and Linda Y. Mokdad, 241–56 Edinburgh: Edinburgh University Press.

O'Brien, Charles. 2019. *Movies, Songs, and Electric Sound*. Bloomington: Indiana University Press.

Petty, Miriam J. 2016. *Stealing the Show: African American Performers and Audiences in 1930s Hollywood*. Berkeley: University of California Press.

Rappler.com. 2018. "A Musical Resurgence Has Hollywood Changing Its Tune." April 19, 2018. https://www.rappler .com/entertainment/news/200624-hollywood-movie -musicals-resurgence.

Sánchez, George J. 1993. *Becoming Mexican American: Ethnicity, Culture, and Identity in Chicano Los Angeles, 1900–1945*. Oxford: Oxford University Press.

Sarris, Andrew. 1977. "The Cultural Guilt of Musical Movies: *The Jazz Singer*, Fifty Years Later." *Film Comment*, September–October, 39–41.

Tusher, Will. 1972. "Cy Feuer Sees Big Rewards in Mid-budget Musical Films." *Hollywood Reporter*, April 6, 1972.

Valle, Victor. 1987. "'La Bamba' May Change Film Marketing." *Los Angeles Times*, July 29, 1987.

Variety. 1966. "Moody Critic Aside, 'Sound of Music' Might Be Out-Blowing Top 'Wind.'" January 19, 1966.

INDEX

Across the Universe (2007), 41

adaptation, the musical and, 6–8, 13, 34, 40, 43

Allen, Woody: *Everyone Says I Love You*, 9, 28–29; *The Purple Rose of Cairo*, 31

All That Heaven Allows (1955), 83–84

All That Jazz (1979), 33–34, 43–44

Altman, Rick, 81, 97

Altman, Robert, 41

American Idol (2002–20), 4

Anders, Allison, 51, 70

Angels with Dirty Faces (1938), 23

Ann-Margret, 32

Applause (1929), 50

archive: Fred Astaire and film, 31; endurance and, 22; hybridity in, 23, 43; *La La Land* as, 20–21; minstrelsy in, 8; movie musical as, 48; musical comedy in, 8, 36; by musical quotations, 22–23, 43; through self-reflexivity, 43; spectatorship and, 8–10; vaudeville in, 8

Ardolino, Emile, 74–75

Armstrong, Gillian, 51

artificiality, 2, 16, 21

Artist, The (2011), 16

Arzner, Dorothy, 69–70

Astaire, Fred: bricolage of, 47, 71; choreography by, 29–30; films archiving, 31; musical quotations with, 9, 24–31

Astaire-Rogers films: quotations of, 9, 24–31; self-reflexive posturing by, 24

"As Time Goes By," 99–100

audiences: archive and spectatorship in, 8–10; *Bamboozled* and, 62, 65–66, 78; in *Begin Again*, 108–9; John Carney removing, 107–8; as diegetic, 61, 66, 73, 108; Jane Feuer on films and, 61, 71; genre revisions through, 78; Spike Lee distancing, 78; musicals incorporating, 21–22; relationship ambiguity with, 73–74; in *Sing Street*, 109–10

audio and visual bridges: Rick Altman on, 97; diegetic

audio and visual bridges (*continued*)
music and, 28, 97, 100; in *Once*, 102–5; *Sing Street* with sound, 95–98

Australia, 9, 51

Avalon, Frankie, 31–32

Babes in Arms (1939), 11, 74–75, 87–88, 90, 109–10

backstage musicals: *Bamboozled* as, 60–62; ethnicity, gender stories in, 11–12; past and present in, 36; race and, 11–12, 62–64; rags-to-riches trajectories in, 55; on women, 50–51

back-studio musical: *The Artist* as, 16; *Hail, Caesar!* as, 16; *Hollywood Shuffle* as, 16; *La La Land* as, 15–17; with self-reflexivity, 16; *Singin' in the Rain* as, 16–17; *A Star Is Born* as, 16

Bacon, Lloyd: *Footlight Parade*, 86–87, 90, 109–10; *The Singing Fool*, 50

Bamboozled (2000), 11–12, 77; audiences and, 62, 65–66, 78; as backstage musical, 60–62; as documentary, 66–67; on entertainment and audiences, 65–66; on race, 62, 68; on US society, 64–66

Band Wagon, The (1953), 38

Barkleys of Broadway, The (1949), 25, 38

Beaumont, Harry, 36, 50, 87–88

Begin Again (2013), 12–13, 79–80, 84–85; audience in, 108–9; band and individuals in, 105; Duran Duran in, 109–10, 112; genre rewritten in, 81–82; music and mediation in, 112–13; playing versus performance in, 107; reality as musical, 100; technology mediating in, 98–101, 113

Berkeley, Busby, 11, 74–75, 87–88, 90, 109–10

Berry, Chuck, 58

Beyond the Lights (2014), 51, 69

Billy Elliot (2000), 9, 31

biopics: as movie musicals, 24, 35–37, 78; rags-to-riches trajectories in, 55

Blondell, Joan, 31–32, 87

Boynton, Lucy, 95

Brecher, Irving, 35

bricolage, 71; with props, 47

Broadway Melody, The (1929), 36, 50, 87–88

Brown, James, 105

"Brown Shoes" (song), 111–12

Buck, Chris, 5, 113

Burden, The (2017), 10, 46–48

Bye Bye Birdie (1963), 32

Cabaret (1972), 43

Cagney, James, 86–87

Camelot (1967), 2

Cameron, Allan, 84

Carney, John: *Begin Again*, 12–13, 79–82, 84–85, 98–101, 105, 107–10, 112–13; *Once*, 12–13, 81, 84–85, 100–105, 107, 112–13; *Sing Street*, 12–13, 81, 83–85, 95–98, 105–7, 109–13

Carolan, Ben, 105

Casablanca (1942), 18–19, 99–100

Cattaneo, Peter, 32

Chamburuka, Percy, 105

Chang, Grace, 46

Chazelle, Damien: *Guy and Madeline on a Park Bench*, 9, 17–19, 32, 42; *La La Land*, 3–6, 9, 15–19, 20–21, 29–30, 42

choreography: by Astaire, 29–30; "Choreography" in *White Christmas*, 38–40; of "Drive It like You Stole It," 110–11; by Pablo Verón, 70

"Choreography" (song-and-dance number), 38–40

Cléo from 5 to 7 (1962), 51, 69

Clooney, Rosemary, 93

Cochran, Eddie, 58

Coen, Ethan, 16

Coen, Joel, 16

Cohan, Steven, 4, 7, 15, 24

collaboration, 105

Columbia Pictures, 59

Columbus, Chris, 23

commercialism, movie musical and, 1–2, 107–8

Commitments, The (1991), 105

communication: listening as, 82, 95–101, 113; music as, 106; technology as, 93

Cooper, Bradley, 49

Cooper, Ralph, 64

Crazy Ex-Girlfriend (2015–19), 4

creating, 101–6, 113

Creekmur, Corey K., 7

Crosby, Bing, 67, 92–93

Crosland, Alan, 1, 11, 50, 52, 55

Cukor, George, 16, 80–81

Cummings, Irving, 62–63

Curtiz, Michael: *Angels with Dirty Faces*, 23; *Casablanca*, 18–19, 99–100; *White Christmas*, 38–40, 92–93

DaCosta, Morton, 11, 52, 93–95

Dailey, Dan, 92

Daldry, Stephen, 9, 31

Dance, Girl Dance (1940), 69–70

Dancer in the Dark (2000), 9, 44–45

"Dancin'" (song-and-dance number), 40–41

Dancing Cavalier, The, 90

Danzón (1991), 51, 69–70

Dash, Julie, 51, 63, 68–70

Davies, Terence, 32

del Toro, Guillermo, 31

Demy, Jacques: *Three Seats for the 26th*, 32; *The Umbrellas of Cherbourg*, 9, 18–19; *The Young Girls of Rochefort*, 9, 31

Denmark, 9

DeSoto, Rosanna, 55

Diamond-Phillips, Lou, 55

diegetic audiences, 61, 66, 73, 108

diegetic music, 28, 97, 100

Dillon, John Francis, 36, 50

Dirty Dancing (1987), 74–75

discrimination, 56–57

Doctor Dolittle (1967), 2

documentary, 66–67, 104

Donen, Stanley, 8, 16–17, 25, 38, 88–90

Down Argentine Way (1940), 62–63

"Drive It like You Stole It" (song-and-dance number), 110–11

Duke Is Tops, The (1938), 64

Duran Duran, 109–10, 112

Durbin, Deanna, 37–38

Dwan, Allan, 91–92

Dyer, Richard, 5, 44

Easter Parade (1948), 31

entertainment: audience convincing for, 61; *Bamboozled* on, 65–66; hybridized musicals for, 34–35, 37–38; movie musicals for, 1, 32, 112; old versus new values in, 32–33; pastiche and hybridity on, 34–35; *That's Entertainment!*, 3

escapism: history of movie musical and, 6–8, 12; John Limon on, 10; movie musicals as, 3–4, 10; popularity versus, 5

ethnicity: backstage musicals and, 11–12; tolerance and, 52, 59, 77–78

Everyone Says I Love You (1996), 9, 28–29

Every Sunday (1936), 37–38

Fairbanks, Douglas, 89

Farmer, Brett, 3

Fee, Matthew J., 97

Feist, Felix E., 37–38

Fellini, Federico, 26–28, 33–34

Feuer, Cy, 2–3

Feuer, Jane, 20; on audiences and films, 61, 71; on couples, 25; on musical and narrative, 21–22; on musicals referencing other musicals, 9; on props, 47

500 Days of Summer (2009), 23

Fleischer, Richard, 2

Fletcher, Anne, 41–42

Flinn, Caryl, 7

folk musicals, 93–94
Footlight Parade (1933), 86–87, 90, 109–10
"For Once in My Life" (song), 99
Fosse, Bob, 33–34, 43–44
France, 9, 31, 51
Frozen (2013), 5, 113–14
Full Monty, The (1997), 32
Funny Girl (1968), 2
Furie, Sidney J., 35

Gabbard, Krin, 4, 55
Gallefant, Edward, 24
Garland, Judy, 37–38, 67, 80, 88; *Guy and Madeline on a Park Bench* quoting, 32; *The Long Day Closes* quoting, 32
gender, 11–12
genre: Jane Feuer on musical, 9; Christian Metz on, 23; revision of, 78, 81–82
Ginger and Fred (1986), 26–28, 33–34
Glee (2009–15), 4
Glorifying the American Girl (1929), 50
Godard, Jean-Luc, 31
Gold Diggers of 1933 (1933), 11
"Good Mornin'" (song-and-dance number), 89
Gopal, Sangita, 7
Grable, Betty, 92
Grace of My Heart (1996), 51, 70

Gracey, Michael, 4–5, 35–36, 52
Graduate, The (1967), 23
Grant, Barry Keith, 21
Grease (1978), 31–32
Greatest Showman, The (2017), 4–5, 35–36, 52, 113–14
Green, Alfred E., 50
Green, Cee Lo, 105
Greenwald, Robert, 31, 40–41
Griffin, Sean, 1, 3, 6–7, 63
Guy and Madeline on a Park Bench (2009), 9, 17–19, 32, 42

Hagen, Jean, 89
Hail, Caesar! (2016), 16
Hairspray (2007), 52
Haley, Jack, Jr., 3
Hamilton, Margaret, 88
Hansard, Glen, 101
Hawks, Howard, 38
Hazanavicius, Michel, 16
Hello, Dolly! (1969), 2
Herman, Mark, 9
Hill, George Roy, 2
Hole, The (1998), 10, 45–46
Holiday, Billie, 35
Holly, Buddy, 56
Hollywood Revue of 1929, The (1929), 87–88
Hollywood Shuffle (1987), 16
Home Alone (1990), 23
home video, 113
Hutton, Betty, 35

hybridity: as anachronistic juxtaposition, 33; for archive, 23, 43; entertainment and, 34–35, 37–38; integration and transformation with, 40; in *Moulin Rouge*, 41; musical films for, 40; silent cinema versus sound cinema, 38; of US society, 58–59

Illusions (1982), 51, 63, 68–69, 70
immigration, 11
Irglová, Markéta, 101
It Blossoms Again (1954), 46

Jackman, Hugh, 35–36
Jagger, Dean, 92
Jameson, Fredric, 33
Japan, 9
jazz music, 38, 42
Jazz Singer, The (1927), 1, 11, 50, 52, 55
Jolson, Al, 50, 67
Jolson Sings Again (1949), 50
Jolson Story, The (1946), 50
Joyrich, Lynn, 84

Kael, Pauline, 2
Kalinak, Kathryn, 7
Kazan, Elia, 23
Kelly, Gene: bricolage of, 47, 71; films quoting, 31–32; *Hello, Dolly!*, 2; *Singin' in the Rain*, 8, 16–17, 25, 38, 88–90
Kennedy, Maria Doyle, 109
Kennedy, Matthew, 3
Kessler, Kelly, 4
Kleiser, Randal, 31–32
Knightley, Keira, 79
Koster, Harry, 92

La Bamba (1987), 11–12, 57, 60, 77; "Lonely Teardrops" in, 58; rags-to-riches trajectories in, 55; "Summertime Blues" in, 58; on US society, 59; on Ritchie Valens, 55, 58–59; "We Belong Together" in, 56; "Well, Let's Go" in, 56
"La Bamba" (song), 55, 58–59
Lady Gaga, 49
Lady Sings the Blues (1972), 35
La La Land (2016), 3–6; as archive, 20–21; Astaire-Rogers films quoted by, 9, 29–30; as back-studio movie, 15–17; *Guy and Madeline* parallel with, 17–19; jazz in crisis in, 42; *Rebel without a Cause* quoted by, 30
Lee, Jennifer, 5, 113
Lee, Spike, 11–12, 60–62, 64–68, 77–78
LeGon, Jeni, 63
LeRoy, Mervyn, 11

Les parapluies de Cherbourg (1964), 9, 18–19
Levin, Henry, 50
Levine, Adam, 108
Levine, Lawrence, 5
Limon, John, 10
listening: for communication, 82, 95–101, 113; music through, 95–101, 113
Little Voice (1998), 9
Lloyd, Phyllida, 41
Logan, Joshua: *Camelot*, 2; *South Pacific*, 52
"Lonely Teardrops" (song), 58
Long Day Closes, The (1992), 32
"Luck Be a Lady" (song), 99
Luhrmann, Baz: *Moulin Rouge*, 41; *Strictly Ballroom*, 9, 75

Ma, Jean, 46
Mambo Girl (1957), 46
Mamma Mia (2008), 41
Mamoulian, Rouben: *Applause*, 50; *Summer Holiday*, 93–94
Mark Taper Forum, 54
Martin, Adrian, 7
Masina, Giulietta, 26
Mastroianni, Marcelo, 26
"Maybe This Time" (song-and-dance number), 43
McKenna, Mark, 95
mediation: John Carney musicals as, 82; devices for, 82–83; music as, 112–13;

musical as, 8, 79, 82, 84; music videos and, 109–10; *Once* and technology, 103; *Sing Street* and, 83, 109–10, 112–13; of technology and musical, 12; by television, 110
Meet Me in St. Louis (1944), 93–94
Metz, Christian, 23
Mexican Americans, 53–60
Miller, Marilyn, 36
Min börda (2017). See *Burden, The* (2017)
Minnelli, Vincente: *The Band Wagon*, 38; *Meet Me in St. Louis*, 93–94
minstrelsy, 31; in archive, 8
Mokdad, Linda K., 7
Moorti, Sujata, 7
Morales, Esai, 55
Moulin Rouge (2001), 41
movie musicals. *See under specific subjects*
Mulvey, Laura, 72
musical comedy, 8, 36, 38
Music Man, The (1962), 11, 52, 93–95
music videos: disruption and challenge by, 112; of flash mobs, 4–5; mediation by, 109–10; as technology, 83, 104, 109–10, 112–13
My Blue Heaven (1950), 92
"My Favorite Things" (song), 44–45

Neale, Steve, 3
Nicholas, Fayard, 62–63
Nicholas, Harold, 62–63
Nichols, Mike, 23
Norðfjörð, Björn, 7
Novaro, Maria, 51

objectification, 53, 69, 72, 80
O'Brien, Charles, 7, 86
O'Connor, Donald, 32, 89
old versus new: in entertainment, 32–33; in movie musical, 48; self-reflexivity, 38; *Step Up* iteration of, 41–42
Once (2007), 12–13, 84–85; with audio and visual bridges, 102–5; band and individuals in, 105; mediation and technology in, 103; music and mediation in, 112–3; music creation in, 101–2; playing versus performance in, 107; reality as movie musical in, 100, 104
One Sings, the Other Doesn't (1977), 51, 69–70
On the Waterfront (1954), 23

Parker, Alan, 105
pastiche: for archive, 43; of entertainment, 34–35; *Moulin Rouge*, 41; as recycling simulation, 33

Pennies from Heaven (1981), 33–34
period films, 35
Petty, Miriam J., 63
Pinkett Smith, Jada, 66–67
Pitch Perfect franchise, 51
playing, 107–14
postmodern films, 33–34
Potter, Sally: audience denial, 78; *The Tango Lesson*, 11–12, 31, 51, 68, 70–78
Prairie Home Companion, A (2006), 41
Prince-Bythewood, Gina, 51, 69
Purple Rose of Cairo, The (1985), 31

quotations: archive of musical, 22–23, 43; of Astaire-Rogers films, 9, 24–31; Gene Kelly films and, 31–32; by movie musicals, 22–23; *Tommy* and, 32

race: as appropriated, 67; backstage musicals and, 11–12, 62–64; *Bamboozled* on, 62, 68; blackness and musicality, 105–6; Jeni LeGon denied roles because of, 63; minstrelsy and, 60–62, 64–68, 78; musicals treatment on, 3–4; used as a prop, 63

Raging Bull (1980), 23

Rainbow, Randy, 4

Ray, Nicholas, 30, 83–84

Rebecca of Sunnybrook Farm (1938), 91–92

Rebel without a Cause (1955), 30, 83–84

Reisner, Charles, 87–88

relationships: audience and ambiguity of, 73–74; *Begin Again* rewriting, 81–82; movie musical and married, 25, 92; *The Tango Lesson* and complex, 72–77; women and, 69–70

Reynolds, Debbie, 87–88

Reynor, Jack, 109

Richardson, J. P. ("The Big Bopper"), 56

"Riddle of the Model, The" (song), 95, 110–11

"Rio" (song), 109–10

Roberta (1935), 29

Rocky Horror Picture Show, The (1975), 5, 33–34

Rogers, Ginger, 9, 24–31

Rooney, Mickey, 88

Ross, Diana, 35

Ross, Herbert, 33–34

Ruffalo, Mark, 79

Russell, Ken, 32

Sally (1929), 36, 50

Sánchez, George J., 57

Sandrich, Mark, 26

Santell, Alfred, 1

Sarris, Andrew, 1

science fiction films, 84

Scorsese, Martin, 23

Scott, Randolph, 91

Seeley, Blossom, 35

Seiter, William A., 29

self-reflexivity: archiving through, 43; Astaire-Rogers films and, 24; back-studio musical and, 16; of movie musical, 20–21, 23, 34; old versus new, 38; for present-day problems, 23; quotation, pastiche, hybridity for, 43; of women filmmakers, 75

Shall We Dance (1996), 9

Shankman, Adam, 52

Shape of Water, The (2017), 31

Sharman, Jim, 5, 33–34

Show Girl (1928), 1

Sidney, George, 32

silent cinema, 67, 86; Douglas Fairbanks in, 89; movie musical slaying, 1, 90–91, 112; *Singin' in the Rain* and, 38, 88–90

Sinatra, Frank, 3, 99

sing-alongs, 113–14

Singing Fool, The (1928), 50

Singin' in the Rain (1952), 8, 25; as back-studio musical, 16–17; "Good Mornin'" in, 89; silent cinema versus

Singin' in the Rain (*continued*)
  sound cinema in, 38,
  88–90
Sing Street (2016), 12–13, 81,
  84–85; audience in, 109–10;
  band and individuals
  in, 105–6; "Drive It like
  You Stole It" in, 110–11;
  mediated circularity in,
  109–10; mediation device
  in, 83; music and mediation
  in, 112–13; playing versus
  performance in, 107; "The
  Riddle of the Model" in, 95,
  110–11; sound bridges in,
  95–98; "Up" in, 95–97
Sirk, Douglas, 83–84
society: *Bamboozled* on US,
  64–66; band and individuals in, 105–6; critique of, 11;
  cultural hybridity in, 58–59;
  discrimination in, 56–57;
  folk musicals and, 93–94;
  individual and public selves
  in, 49–50; Mexican Americans in, 53–55; musicals
  as, 8, 77, 84; musicals with
  tolerance and, 51–53; sing-
  alongs and, 113–14; technology and family life, 93–95;
  television and, 91–92; white
  male subjectivity in, 10–11
solace: in *The Burden*, 10,
  46–48; in *Cabaret*, 43
Somebody Loves Me (1956), 35

Song Is Born, A (1948), 38
Sound of Music, The (1965),
  1, 10; Pauline Kael on, 2;
  "My Favorite Things" in,
  44–45; sing-alongs for,
  113–14
South Pacific (1958), 52
So You Think You Can Dance
  (2005–20), 4
spectatorship, 8–10
Star! (1968), 2
Star Is Born, A (1954), 16,
  80–81
Star Is Born, A (2018), 49
Starstruck (1982), 51, 69–70
Step Up: 2006 film, 41–42;
  franchise, 51
Stevens, George, 26, 29–30
Stone, Andrew L., 63–64
Stormy Weather (1943), 63–64
*Story of Vernon and Irene
  Castle, The*, 24–25, 30–31
Strictly Ballroom (1992), 9, 75
Summer Holiday (1948), 93–94
Summer Stock (1950), 74–75
"Summertime Blues" (song),
  58
Suo, Masayuki, 9
Swing Time (1936), 26, 29–30

Tango Lesson, The (1997),
  11–12, 31, 51, 68, 78; complex
  relationships in, 72–77;
  female desires met in,
  70–72; females over males

in, 70; men controlling women in, 75–76

Taymor, Julie, 41

Teatro Campesino, 53–54

technology: *Begin Again* mediation with, 98–101, 113; for communication, 93; devices for mediation, 82–83; family life integrating, 93–95; mediation and, 12; mediation devices, 82–83; musicals reckoning with, 85, 90; Charles O'Brien on musicals and, 7, 86; sing-alongs using, 113–14; talkies versus vaudeville, 86–87

television: *American Idol*, 4; *Crazy Ex-Girlfriend*, 4; family and community, 91–92; *Glee*, 4; mediation by, 110; in musicals, 92–93; musical variety shows, 60; *My Blue Heaven* incorporating, 92; *So You Think You Can Dance*, 4; threat by, 91; *The Voice*, 4; *White Christmas* incorporating, 92

Temple, Shirley, 67, 91

That's Entertainment! (1974), 3

Thoroughly Modern Millie (1967), 2

Three Seats for the 26th (1988), 32

tolerance, 51, 53; ethnicity and, 52, 59, 77–78; musicals on, 77

Tommy (1975), 32–34

Top Hat (1935), 26

Top of the Pops, 109

Townsend, Robert, 16

Trois places pour le 26 (1988), 32

"Trolley Song, The" (song), 94

Tsai Ming-liang, 10, 45–46

Tusher, Will, 3

20th Century Fox, 63

Umbrellas of Cherbourg, The (1964), 9, 18–19

United Kingdom, 9

United States (US): *La Bamba* and society of, 59; *Bamboozled* and society of, 64–66; Mexican Americans in, 53–60; musicals from outside of, 9, 18, 24; women and musicals outside of, 51; women filmmakers outside of, 69

"Up" (song), 95–97

Valdez, Luis: audience identification promoted by, 78; *La Bamba*, 11–12, 53–60, 77; Teatro Campesino, 53–54; *Zoot Suit*, 53–55, 57, 59

Valens, Ritchie, 55, 58–59

Valle, Victor, 59

Varda, Agnès, 51, 69–70
Variety, 2, 87
vaudeville, 31, 35–36; in archive, 8; talkies' technology versus, 86–87
Verón, Pablo, 70–72
Viva Las Vegas (1964), 32
Voice, The (2011–), 4
Von Bahr, Niki Lindroth, 10, 46–48
von Trier, Lars, 9, 44–45
Von Zerneck, Danielle, 55

Walsh-Peelo, Ferdia, 95
Walters, Charles: *The Barkleys of Broadway*, 25, 38; *Summer Stock*, 74–75
Warner Bros., 49, 53–54
Wayans, Damon, 60
Webb, Marc, 23
Webb, Millard, 50
"We Belong Together" (song), 56
"Well, Let's Go" (song), 56
"Wells Fargo Wagon, The" (song-and-dance number), 94–95
Westley, Helen, 91
"What Do You Do with a General?" (song), 92–93
White Christmas (1954): "Choreography" in, 38–40; television incorporated in, 92; "What Do You Do with a General?" in, 92–93

white male subjectivity, 10–11
Wilson, Dooley, 99–100
Winninger, Charles, 87
Wise, Robert: *The Sound of Music*, 1–2, 10, 44–45, 113–14; *Star!*, 2
Woman Is a Woman, A (1961), 31
women: desires met by, 70–72; films and relationships of, 69–70; as idealized objects, 68–69; men controlling, 10–11, 69, 75–76; movie musicals on and by, 50–51; as non-US filmmakers, 69; self-reflexivity on filmmakers and, 75; *The Tango Lesson* privileging, 70–77
Wonder, Stevie, 99
working-class intolerance: *Babes in Arms* on, 11; *Gold Diggers of 1933* on, 11
Wyler, William, 2

Xanadu (1980), 31, 40–41

Young Girls of Rochefort, The (1967), 9, 31
YouTube: *La La Land* and *The Greatest Showman* on, 4–5; Randy Rainbow on, 4

Ziegfeld shows, 36
zombie films, 84
Zoot Suit (1981), 53–55, 57, 59

ABOUT THE AUTHOR

Desirée J. Garcia is an associate professor in the Latin American, Latino, and Caribbean Studies Program and an affiliate in the Film and Media Studies Department at Dartmouth College. She is the author of *The Migration of Musical Film: From Ethnic Margins to American Mainstream* (Rutgers University Press, 2014). She has also published numerous articles on the transnational histories of musical film, ethnic performance, and spectatorship in the *Quarterly Review of Film and Video, Film History,* the *Journal of American Ethnic History,* and *Frontiers: A Journal of Women's Studies.* She has a PhD in American Studies from Boston University and BA in history from Wellesley College. Garcia has also worked as an associate producer for *American Experience* (PBS) and starred in the first feature film by the director Damien Chazelle (*La La Land*), an original musical called *Guy and Madeline on a Park Bench* (2009).